HAPPINESS REHAB

8 Creative Steps to a More Joyful Life

Jennifer Archer

Mary L. Schramski, Ph.D.

Table of Contents

Dedication

To all who seek creativity and a full, joyous life.

Welcome to Happiness Rehab

As the authors of this book, we're happy to have you join us on this journey. Happiness Rehab is an effective, creative workshop that will teach you about your creativity and cultivate your happiness. We developed this program because we know creativity and happiness are connected, and we are dedicated to helping people become more creative and more satisfied with their lives. We have experienced, firsthand, full creative lives and we know that if approached correctly, creativity can bring anyone more happiness.

What Will This Workshop Do For You?

If you have trouble recalling a time when you were creative, you aren't alone. Today's lifestyles are hectic and stressful. The sort of happiness and creativity you experienced as a child and were meant to enjoy forever has probably disappeared.

Most people long for creative outlets and the happiness they bring, and you are probably no different. With each Step in this workshop, we will guide you through fun "Practices" that will help you remember when creativity played an active role in your life. These Practices will inspire your creativity and begin to bring you added joy. We'll also show you how to overcome fears and manage your creative time. You'll learn to use your mind as a creative tool and reap the benefits of solving problems faster. You'll find that you will become more alert and aware. In short, you are going to rediscover your imaginative power and begin to live life with all the happiness you were meant to have.

How to Use This Book

Creativity is a wonderful gift. People learn about the creative process and practice using it in many unique ways. With that in mind, there are no hard and fast rules when it comes to working your way through the Steps of this book. Just read through each Step with an open mind. However, to get the most out of your experience, we suggest that you participate in the Practices and keep a Creative Happiness Journal. Buy a spiral notebook to record your Practice answers and journal entries. Or purchase something fancier if that inspires you.

The finely-tuned Practices we have developed for this workshop are designed to challenge and encourage your imagination. They are found in the text or at the end of each Step.

After completing each Step, write in your journal about your thoughts and experiences and note your newly-found creativity and happiness as it unfolds. Voice your hopes, your expectations, your discoveries and even your fears. Most importantly don't worry about the correctness of your journal. Spelling, grammar and neatness don't matter. Simply write down what you're thinking and experiencing. We have included Creative Happiness Journal prompts to inspire you; however, if you choose not to use them, that's fine.

As a guide, our Practice responses and journal entries are placed within the text of each Step for your immediate reference. And we've also included a few responses here and there from others who have participated in this workshop in the past.

This is your workshop – enjoy it! Let's take the first Step.

Meet Your Facilitators

We're going to be spending a lot of time with one another and learning together as we take this creative happiness journey. Before we get started, let's make introductions.

Jennifer (Workshop Facilitator)
My name is Jennifer Archer and I'm excited that you're here and thrilled to be presenting this workshop to you along with my friend Mary Schramski.

I believe strongly in the power of creativity, and I can't wait to share with you what I've learned about the topic through both study and firsthand experience. When I was ten years old, I made up my mind that I was going to be a writer. But then I grew up, became "sensible," and earned a business degree with a minor in accounting instead.

I spent many years trying to find my way through a confusing maze of debits and credits before realizing that, for me, accounting was no more sensible than becoming a World Federation wrestler! That was sometime around 1993, and I celebrated my epiphany by enrolling in a creative writing course. During the first class, I felt energized and excited – like I'd rediscovered a part of myself that I'd lost. That was probably the first time I realized the connection between creativity and happiness. I began nurturing my creativity; I was determined never to lose sight of it again.

Five years after taking that class, I sold my first novel, *Body and Soul*, and went on to publish several novels for adults and numerous non-fiction books and articles. I've been a finalist twice for Romance Writers of America's Golden Heart award, a finalist for the Rita Award, and a nominee for a Romantic Times Bookclub Magazine Reviewer's Choice Award. My debut Young Adult novel, *Through Her Eyes*, was published in April, 2011 by Harper Teen, and my second novel for young adults, *The Shadow Girl*, is scheduled for publication in April, 2013.

I've taught creativity and creative writing in a college classroom, and I've presented numerous talks and workshops on the subject for educators, writers' organizations and bookstores. Each time I do, I'm struck by the energy in the room. People are hungry for creativity! I'm convinced it's as essential for a fulfilled life as love and security. So I hereby congratulate you on your decision to live your fullest life – one complete with creative happiness.

Mary (Workshop Facilitator)

I'm Mary Schramski and I'm excited you've decided to join our workshop. Jennifer Archer and I have worked on many projects together, but honestly, this is my favorite one because I love it when creatives progress through these Steps and become more creative and happy. What a joy! And I always learn from participants; it's a wonderful gift for any facilitator when we learn together.

My professional creative life began when I wrote my first short story at 10. I've created with F. Scott Fitzgerald while reading his novel, *The Great Gatsby*, probably fifty times. Then, while matriculating through my English degree, I realized I was intensely interested in creativity: how people create, why, and how to enhance people's creative journey. When I began teaching English this interest grew as I observed my students at their happiest when I promoted their creativity.

After completing my Masters Degree in Education and English, my interest ignited even more – I wanted to make my courses a creative heaven for my students. I developed many methods to enhance their creativity, and as I did this I realized I was happier when I created, too.

Bingo!

I focused on Creativity – the psychology of it, education and creative writing – while pursuing my doctorate. I connected creativity with joy and happiness and observed how content creative people could be.

I began ghosting books and editing for others after publishing thirteen books. Then while talking with Jennifer one day, we decided to create this *Happiness Rehab* workshop. Our main goal is to share this method with the world, one creative person at a time.

So welcome to a new world, the world of happy creativity.

Step 1

Understanding How the Creative Mind Works

YOU Are Creative

Let's start by recognizing a fact:

You are a creative person.

Read that sentence again. It's true, but right now you may not believe it.

We have met *many* people who think they aren't creative. Some even freeze from nerves when asked to use their imagination. Most of these people view creativity as mysterious and out of reach – a precious, highly-coveted treasure that only a few possess. They envy creative people and want what they have, not realizing they already have it. Yet, with a little encouragement, each and every one of these people eventually discovers his or her creative abilities, and so can you. You simply need to learn more about your creative self to bring it out of hiding.

To begin demystifying creativity, let's consider an analogy: In the *Wizard of Oz,* the Tin Man dreams of having a heart, the Scarecrow cries over being brainless, the Cowardly Lion longs for courage, and Dorothy wants to live in a happy place. All these characters mistakenly believe these traits exist *outside* of themselves, far off in the Emerald City. However each character soon discovers the truth: what they want already exists *inside* of them and always has. They just need to believe.

The same is true of you. Your creativity already exists inside of you, and you can begin to uncover it by believing it's there. To do this you need to open your mind to the power of your imagination. If you do, we predict that soon you'll be drawing upon that power and using it in your daily life in ways that will bring you more satisfaction.

Understanding Your Creative Flow

How many times have you read a book and become so engrossed in the story that it was as if you were experiencing it along with the characters? When this happened, you were creating in conjunction with the author who wrote the book. You took the author's words and painted a picture in your mind. You heard the characters' voices and experienced the other senses brought to life by the words on the page. During this time, you didn't think about problems and time sped by.

If you aren't a reader, perhaps you've experienced this same phenomenon while painting a model airplane, decorating a room, pasting items into a scrapbook, cooking or taking photographs. You were in the creative flow.

Creative flow is that mesmerizing feeling that happens when you are caught up in your imagination. And it is one reason people value creativity. Everyone loves that effortless, yet highly focused state of being that carries us away to another world where hours pass in a flash, everyday problems don't exist, and boredom and unhappiness evaporate. Plus all self-consciousness and the hard work of protecting our egos – an effort in which we all engage – disappears.

No little white pill could produce more joy than the flow of creation.

The Creativity/Happiness Connection

To better understand how creativity can bring more happiness into your life, let's talk about the ways in which happiness and creativity are intertwined.

All people are born with the desire and the ability to make something new. If creativity stops being an active part of your life, the world can start to feel like a humdrum place. That's because, as humans, our greatest pleasure comes from being innovative. Doing so stimulates the pleasure center in our brains, and pleasure makes us happy. When you experience creative pleasure, it spills over into all of the other facets of your life. The creativity and happiness connection is as simple as that.

Existential psychologist Rollo May states, "We self-actualize through creativity." Also, the end result of the creative act changes our environment, our quality of life, and our existence. Even when we see others create, we feel a measure of joy. Creativity is one powerful force, a learning tool. And we become the receptors.

So why is it such a struggle for some people to tap into their imaginative force? If we are all creative, and creativity brings happiness, shouldn't it be easy to be innovative?

There are three basic reasons why it's difficult for many adults to be creative:

They believe creativity should be effortless.
They are not awake to their surroundings.
They have lost their ability to be childlike.

The Effortless Creativity Myth

Most of us have been led to believe that creative inspiration should be easy. You might think that if you're truly a creative person, you should be able to sit back, close your eyes, and your muse will visit. *Voila!* Just like that, original ideas will suddenly abound and happiness will ride into your life like a white knight to the rescue.

This myth probably began because that is often exactly how the creative process *appears* to take place. Note the word "*appears*." Creativity *doesn't* happen effortlessly. While it's true that your mind is always working creatively, your imaginative thoughts and ideas must be acknowledged and nurtured if they're to thrive. And the way to acknowledge and nurture them is to be mentally present and aware of your creative process.

In other words, if you take the time to notice things around you and are not on autopilot all the time, you'll be more creative.

Awakening to Your Surroundings

It's a fact that most people maneuver through life in a semi-daze. It's an easy state to fall into when you're worried about bills, work, family obligations and life in general. Yet you must break out of this conditioning if you want to live creatively. So let's practice being more aware.

Step 1 Practice: Awareness
Right now just listen. What do you hear? Try closing your eyes and going deeper to notice what sounds exist beneath the obvious. Then, in your notebook, document where you are and list three sounds you noticed.

Next, take a moment to study your hands. See if you can notice at least one thing about them you've never realized before and write it in your notebook.

Jennifer's Responses:
I am in a coffee shop and I hear:
1. A constant hissing white noise of the air conditioner beneath the music playing and the murmurs of people talking.
2. The scrape of metal chair legs on the concrete floor.
3. My own breathing.

While studying my hands, I noticed:
1. I have tiny, thick, smooth calluses on my palms at the base of my middle and ring fingers.

Mary's Responses:
I am in a library and hear:
1. The whirling rush of a floor polisher.
2. A soft whisper of a woman's voice.
3. A child giggling.

While studying my hands, I noticed:
1. My nails are gently rounded.

It's always amazing to read workshop participants' first responses. Noises go on all around us constantly, but we often unconsciously tune out all but the loudest sounds. And we see our hands every day – they're nothing new – yet almost everyone is able to find one thing about his or her hands that they've never noticed before.

This Practice offers a tiny example of how you can be more aware of the things around you every day and start to become more creative. Awareness is the source of creativity!

Our Lost Ability to be Childlike

Creativity comes naturally to babies and children – they play with everything within reach – even their hands and feet. They pretend and make up stories, living in their own imaginative worlds. And you were no different when you were a child.

Unfortunately, outside forces – namely adults – began to temper your creative spirit when you were still a baby. It's ironic, isn't it? Adults value creativity, yet in many ways they discourage it in their youngsters.

When you were a toddler, it's likely the people who cared for you took objects from you that you were chewing, shaking and exploring, and you were told, "Don't touch." Then as you grew older, those well-meaning adults – perhaps teachers and/or parents – instructed you to "act your age," "quit daydreaming," "get your head out of the clouds," and you did, albeit reluctantly.

With age, your responsibilities also increased. As each year passed, you had more homework, more household chores, then a job. Suddenly there were bills to pay, meetings to attend, appointments to schedule, and people who depended upon you. Without realizing it, you stopped playing, pretending and imagining and became a "responsible grown-up." Without your attention, your imagination folded up like a tent and tucked itself away.

However, you can coax it out again.

In Step 1 Practice we encouraged you to be childlike by asking you to study your hands for a moment. (If you watch a baby or child long enough, you will catch them staring at their hands.) In Step 2 we will delve deeper into your childlike, creative self, and you will learn how to use that part of your personality to become more creative and infuse more happiness into your life.

The Tortured Artist Myth – Don't Believe It

Before we move on to Step 2, we should address an issue that is bound to come up for at least a few of you. Occasionally workshop participants challenge our claim that creativity breeds happiness by pointing out that many famous artists and musicians and other creative types were known to be depressed or filled with angst. Some people even express fear that if they are "too creative," they may begin to experience mental anguish, as well.

Fact: The Tortured Artist persona is a myth.

This myth more than likely took root because well-known musicians, writers and other types of artists get a lot of press, and if they're battling internal demons they receive even more attention.

No profession is exempt from angst, depression or other mental disorders, but most are not viewed under a microscope as are many artistic occupations. In fact, a

2009 article in *Psychology Today* ranked physicians as the professionals with the highest suicide rate. Yet, because the private lives of physicians aren't as highly visible to the general public as are the private lives of artists, we aren't as aware of their personal struggles.

To further debunk the tortured artist myth, let's consider which came first – the art or the depression – for the unfortunate creative folks that *do* suffer from extreme mental anguish. Many troubled people turn to creativity as an outlet or reprieve from their distress, rather than their distress stemming from their involvement with creativity. In his book *The Dynamics of Creation*, British psychiatrist Anthony Storr agrees with our assessment. He indicates that creating soothes the artist's soul.

Connecting to your creative self won't doom you. Quite the opposite – using your creative energy will connect you more closely to the beauty of your world and bring you a sense of peace, contentment and happiness.

Creative Happiness Journal Prompt

After you read our journal entries, write in your own journal. Remember – don't worry about correctness. The most important part of writing in your journal is to feel at ease as you jot down your thoughts. Here's a prompt if you need an idea to guide you: Write about your experience with creativity and your thoughts about Step 1.

Mary's Creative Happiness Journal

I've always intuitively known that happiness and creativity are connected. When I'm writing, decorating or even cutting out snowflakes for my Christmas tree, I feel happy. Yes, trying to be creative can be stressful, but when I'm in that creative flow there is no place I'd rather be. I think that's why I'm so happy – because I create all the time and for years I've understood that if I'm not attached to my creativity, then I'm not as happy as I should be.

When I was a kid, the happiest place for me was art class and I can't even draw a straight line. Another thing creativity has done for me is to make me appreciate life more. I stop every day and look out the window at the sunrise and imagine different ways I could describe it. I take deep breaths and enjoy the sparkle of the sun on the sidewalk, the music that I love, and the voices I hear. But staying connected to my creative self is work sometimes because I'm so busy. I go through an entire day and then realize I haven't stopped to just enjoy our world. Writing this book has been a big reminder. And as I've been writing I realize that creativity brings me as much joy as love does. I've increased my photography, started listening to music more and have really begun to understand the process even more than I did before.

The most creative I've ever been was when I was writing my novel, *The Lighthouse*. I'd written novels for years and felt the creative flow many times, but not like I did while writing *The Lighthouse*. When I wrote that book, I was relaxed and confident, two big components for a creative life.

Jennifer's Creative Happiness Journal
I definitely lost touch with my creative side when I was

in high school and college, and during the early years of my marriage. Prior to high school, I was involved with music, playing the clarinet in my junior high band. And I wrote short stories and poems just for the pleasure it brought me. Then when I started high school, I quit band because it wasn't "cool." If I could go back and talk to my 15 year old self, I'd give her a good shake for that. The truth is, quitting band didn't make me any cooler and I had a lot less fun. I also quit writing stories unless they were assigned, mostly because I became so busy with other things – school and a part-time job, friendships and a boyfriend. I had always wanted to be a writer, but I let that dream go, too, because I didn't know how to begin to pursue it. I didn't know any writers I could talk to, and I had this mistaken notion that all writers lived in places like New York City or Europe, not in smallish, dusty West Texas towns.

It wasn't until I was in my early thirties with children that I discovered that my local community college offered a creative writing class taught by a published author. My old dream woke up and nudged me. That was almost 20 years ago and I haven't stopped writing since, so I know firsthand that while creative instincts might go dormant for awhile, they don't die. They can be revived.

Even during the past 20 years that I've been actively pursuing a creative life again, I've fallen prey to the forces that tend to stifle creativity from time to time. Mostly, I get busy with all the mundane responsibilities of life and forget to pay attention to the world around me. This usually doesn't last long, because I make a conscious effort to remain aware. One way I do this is to constantly ask myself "what if." *What if I lived in that little isolated house on the side of the highway I always drive by on my way to our cabin in the mountains; what would my life be like? What if I could step into this old photograph of my grandfather when he was a kid and discover what life was like during that time and what was going on with him at the moment the picture was shot? What if, in that magazine article I read about the woman who gave up her baby for adoption 35 years ago, instead of her daughter showing up and finding her, her grandson did and told her that her daughter was dead?*

Those last two "what ifs" actually resulted in ideas for two of my novels – *Through Her Eyes*, and *The Me I Used To Be*.

When I disconnect from my creativity even for a short time, my life feels *off*, like something's out of whack and I'm no longer in balance. It's true that creating isn't effortless, but the effort it takes makes life so much more colorful and interesting.

Step 2

Reconnecting With Your Creativity

Pushing Through Roadblocks

Fortunately, the old cliché "use it or lose it" doesn't apply to creativity. As we've already mentioned, your imagination is always ready and waiting for you to push the 'reconnect' button and make creativity an active part of your daily life again. It's all a matter of learning how to get started.

We meet people all the time who've been detached from their creative instincts for so long that whenever they consider trying to make contact again, a mental wall automatically goes up. So how can you begin to break through the roadblocks that are holding you back from the creative life you desire?

The following Practice can help crack any barrier you might face.

Step 2 Practice: Identifying Obstacles

In your notebook, answer the following prompt by listing two things that are keeping you from being more creative. Don't think too hard, simply write whatever pops into your mind first.

Prompt: **I'm not as creative as I would like to be**

because . . .

Read your responses and think about what you stated. This is an illuminating exercise and a healing one because your responses reveal what is holding you back. And once a problem is identified, you can get to work on solving it. Here are our responses to the above prompt:

Jennifer's Responses:
I'm not as creative as I would like to be because:
1. I'm afraid I'll fail, and then I will feel I've wasted my time.
2. I've been disappointed lately when a few of my creative ideas haven't worked out exactly as I'd envisioned.

Mary's Responses:
I'm not as creative as I would like to be because:
1. At times I feel like a blank slate without chalk. I want to create but nothing is there.
2. I'm so busy – where would I find the time to be more creative?

Do you relate to either of our responses? Other common problems people often list are: Embarrassment of what people will think. Fear of success or failure. Confusion about what or how to create.

Your responses might contain one or more of these concerns, or others unique to you. However, the next Practice will teach you ways to get past any blockade you encounter on the road to a more creative life.

Remembering Yourself as a Creative Person

One way to tackle the issues holding you back and start to reconnect with your creativity is to pinpoint an interest you might be passionate about and then participate in it. The best way to uncover your passion is to remember the way you played as a child.

Step 2 Practice: Childhood Play

Think back to when you were a child and played, not team sports coached by an adult or any type of lessons, but when you or your friends were free to create your own fun.

Write short Responses in your notebook to the following questions:

1. What was your favorite play activity(s)?
2. Did you prefer playing alone, with a friend, or with a group?
3. Which did you enjoy more -- playing inside or outside?
4. The activities you enjoyed were (a) Active – for example, board games, sports or making paper dolls. (b) Pretend -- for example, making up stories with dolls or playing "cops and robbers."

Your responses to these questions provide clues that will help you uncover the creative passions buried inside you. They also prove you were once a very creative person. If you liked playing alone, you might like to create in solitude. If you loved groups, your creativity might soar with others around. If you preferred being inside, gardening might not become your passion, but something like sewing or decorating might.

Maybe you loved playing with an Easy Bake Oven, were good at decorating the little cakes and were the hit of the neighborhood for your creations. Now that you're an adult, you might enjoy taking a cooking class.

Or maybe you made plastic jewelry, stringing together multi-colored beads. Or you might've colored pictures and gave them away. These childhood interests indicate that you might enjoy taking an art or jewelry-designing class.

When Mary was a girl, she loved dressing her Barbie doll, organizing Barbie's clothes and shoes, and making new outfits out of tissue paper. Now she enjoys fashion as a hobby, and feels happy when she pulls together a great outfit or someone asks her to help them with their wardrobe.

Jennifer loved playing alone with her dolls and stuffed animals and making up little soap operas about what was going on in their imaginary world – the precursor of her passion for writing.

Look again at your Practice Responses and imagine how you could turn one of your childhood pastimes into a creative outlet now that you're an adult. Allow what you learn from this Practice to inspire you, and acknowledge that you were – and still are – creative. Then rediscover the fun of a past activity, or explore something altogether new. Set aside some play time today and rejoice in the happiness it brings.

Exploriments

Another way to rediscover an old creative passion, or to form a new one, is to explore various creative outlets in a hands-on way.

We call these "exploriments" because you both explore and experiment. Considering trying a new exploriment every month until something clicks and you know you've found the creative passion you wish to pursue.

Let this short list inspire you to come up with your own unique ideas for activities to try.

1. If you don't have a camera, buy a cheap disposable one and take off on a photo-taking mission. Snap shots around your neighborhood, the mall, a park, a cemetery, an amusement park. Or simply take photos inside your house or your own backyard.

2. Buy a new cookbook or pull out an old one you seldom use. Find a recipe for something unlike anything you've ever made before. Assemble the ingredients and utensils you need, tie on an apron and get cookin!

3. Rearrange and redecorate a room using furniture, knickknacks, lamps, pictures, etc., that you already have on hand. Position furniture in a way you never considered before. Combine items you never thought about putting together – a pillow on a

sofa, a picture above a chair, a flower arrangement on a table. Experiment!

4. Take a field trip to a hobby store and wander up and down the aisles. Explore the artificial flower department. Touch knitting and crochet yarn. Feel the texture of upholstery and clothing fabrics. Scoop loose beads for making jewelry into your hands. Shake tiny bottles of artist oil paint and look at all the brushes. Take note of where you linger the longest, what catches your eye, and what keeps drawing you back for another look.

5. Refinish a piece of wooden furniture. If you don't have one available, browse a few yard sales or go to a flea market to find one. To help you get started, you might read a 'how-to' manual for refinishing furniture. These can be found at craft or hardware stores.

6. If there's a community college or a university nearby where you live, find out if they offer continuing education courses. Colleges that do often hold these at night so people who work during the day can attend. Classes might include fishing fly tying, photography, calligraphy, creative writing, painting, quilting, woodworking, and many other options. Choose something that appeals to you, sign up, and give it a try.

7. Buy an instrument and take music lessons. This

doesn't have to be an expensive endeavor. Find a used instrument at a music store or online through sites like Craigslist. Then check out the free lessons offered for your particular instrument on YouTube.

8. Write a poem, a short story or the lyrics to a song. If you want guidance, buy a book on creative writing or songwriting to help you get started.

Connecting Creativity and Happy Times

Since we've now established you are a creative person, the next key component to being more so is recognizing the happiness you experience when you create.

You may not realize it, but you have experienced creative happiness many times in your life. Maybe you've shot a great photograph that captured the subject in a unique way. Or perhaps you once thought of a distinctive way to maximize the cabinet space in your kitchen, or saw autumn leaves on the ground and realized they looked just like a painting.

Have you ever arranged flowers in a vase? Built a tree house? Decorated a room? You've undoubtedly engaged in one of these or any number of other creative activities, and when you did, you felt happy and proud, didn't you?

When Jennifer was nine or ten years old, she taught herself to play a Peter, Paul and Mary song, "Oh, Rock My Soul," on the ukulele. She really got into learning the different chords from a manual. She was in the creative flow while she practiced, and put her own spin on the tune. Once she could play it through from start to finish, she was thrilled with the sense of achievement she felt.

Mary recently designed an entertainment center for her living room without having any design experience, then had it built. Now, every time she sees it, she not only feels creative, she's delighted by what she accomplished.

As you can see, feelings of satisfaction and joy go hand-in-hand with creation. No matter what creative experiences you've had, they are imaginative and interesting and possess the potential to bring you more happiness because they're unique to you. They prove that you are truly a creative person.

Learning from Creative People You Admire

You probably admire a few people who have managed to stay creatively connected, even as adults. They continually practice creating, and you can start now to do the same by following their lead.

These people often have creative occupations. They may make their living as artists, actors, photographers, musicians, decorators, architects, jewelry-makers, soap makers, or even gardeners. However, some work in more "logical" occupations while sustaining their creativity through an active hobby.

So how do they preserve their creative instincts while growing up, in spite of increasing obligations and tempering from outside forces?

There is no single answer to this question. Some might have had parents who actively encouraged their imaginative pursuits. Others may have been fortunate to have teachers who praised their creative abilities. And some may be more strongly inclined through genetics toward artistic pursuits than the typical person. Whatever the case:

They understand creativity is NOT effortless.

They stay aware of their surroundings.

They remain childlike in ways relating to creativity.

Step 2 Practice: A Creative Person You Admire

You may personally know at least one really creative person you admire. If not, ask your friends if they know someone you could interview. Jot down his/her name in your journal and what he/she creates. Then call or email this person and ask if you can meet face-to-face.

You might ask the following questions, or come up with your own:

1. How do you keep your life in the creative zone?
2. Do you believe creativity is effortless?
3. Are you aware of your surroundings in a creative way? If so, explain.
4. Explain how you are playful when creating.

After the interview, think about the answers you received and write in your Creative Happiness Journal about why you think this person has remained creative and how you might emulate him or her.

Mary's Interview:

Name: Tiffany

1. What do you create? *Note cards, tiaras, a glamorous lifestyle.*
2. How do you keep your life in the creative zone? *I am aware. I open my eyes and look. A tree just isn't a tree, it's dressed in a bikini or a ball gown. I see this all the time.*
3. Do you believe creativity is effortless? *Some is, some is not. To me creativity is like a light. Sometimes the light is on, sometimes I have to flip it on. I tell myself to be creative, take a deep breath and relax.*
4. Are you aware of your surroundings in a creative way? *Yes!* Explain: *I'm a sensuous person – I love the senses,smells, taste, sight. It's all amazing to me.*
5. Explain how you are playful when creating? *It is the best feeling in the world. I feel like a child. I'm in the zone where there is no time, no hunger – no high like it. I can't even imagine not having an idea.*

Jennifer's Interview

Name: Linda

1. What do you create? *I write novels.*
2. How do you keep your life in the creative zone? *Writing is my full time job now, but it wasn't always that way. I used to have a full-time job in the corporate world. During that time, my passion for writing and creating stories kept me in the creative zone. I loved writing and I totally wanted to get published and write full time. The old cliché "where there's a will,*

there's a way," is true. I was busy, but I made time to write. I wrote in the a.m. before work and on my lunch hour. If I made every light right, it took me 12 minutes to get home and that gave me half an hour to write at lunch.

3. Do you believe creativity is effortless? *Sometimes it is effortless but sometimes it's not. It really depends on where you are in your life. For instance, writing is hard but sometimes I'm so driven by the story that the words flow out easily. Other times, I want to beat my head on the keyboard.*

4. Are you aware of your surroundings in a creative way? *Sometimes. Not all the time.* Explain: *Ideally, I would be all the time but sometimes regular life intervenes. I find that if I relax my mind, I often notice something in the world that sparks an idea for the story I'm writing.*

5. Explain how you are playful when creating. *My mind is usually cluttered with all kinds of information and things I need to do. But when I'm writing, all of that goes away. If you can open up your mind, you can open up your creativity.*

Creative Happiness Journal Prompt

Write in your journal about your journey with the workshop so far. Here's a prompt if you need an idea to guide you: How do you/can you better connect with your creative self?

Mary's Creative Happiness Journal

I have always been connected to my creative self. I remember making up stories when I was five in the back of my mother's Oldsmobile as we sped along the sunny California highways. For that matter, any place became my fantasy world. At bath time I was at the Malibu beach riding waves. At night I told myself stories to go to sleep. As I grew older, I created things. One time I tore apart my underwear and made a bathing suit that wasn't wearable – but it was something I was proud of.

The Christmas after my parents divorced, my mother was too distraught to buy a Christmas tree so I made one out of pink tissue and cardboard tubes. I used to draw flowers and tiny nymphs under them, though I wasn't all that artistically inclined. And since 7th grade I always signed up for art class -six years of art classes and I still can't draw a straight line. But I didn't care. I was happy in art class.

I am a balanced right-brain/left-brain. I love thinking logically about finance and science. I used to tutor biology in college and love when facts fit together like puzzle pieces. However when I flunked high school algebra, it was because I was in "love" with the boy who sat in front of me, couldn't stop dreaming about him, and I also couldn't stop wondering, "But why does X equal Y."

One creative activity has always been consistent for me: writing. I wrote my first short story when I was twelve. Before that I was enthralled with Dick and Jane. I kept journals, wrote non-fiction and fiction. Realizing that I was a writer was the happiest day of my life. And knowing that I could research creativity and help people become more creative was my grand achievement.

Jennifer's Creative Happiness Journal

There's a theory that the right side of the brain controls creativity and the left side controls logic, and it's said that often in people, one side is more developed than the other. Looking back at my childhood, I believe I was born more naturally right-brained than left-brained. I loved making up stories and acting them out. I also loved music. Besides teaching myself to play a couple of songs on the ukulele, I started playing the clarinet in band in 4th grade. (Right brained activities). I was terrible at math and science (both left brained activities).

I remember in first or second grade, my dad sitting with me at the kitchen table helping me with math homework. 'What's 2 + 6?' he asked me. 'Eight,' I answered. 'Correct,' he said. 'So what's 6 + 2?' I remember getting a panicky feeling and saying, 'I don't know. My teacher hasn't taught us the sixes yet.' It's a funny story now, but even simple numbers like that were a confusing mystery to me then. Ironically, I went to college and majored in business with a minor in accounting, in spite of being number-challenged. I don't know . . . maybe I was trying to prove to my father that I could understand math. Or maybe I was trying to prove something to myself. But I do know that accounting was the absolute wrong occupation for me. I was a terrible accountant! Thank goodness I found my way back to my dream of writing.

Funny thing, working on this book has uncovered my old desire to play music. I'm finding myself thinking more about learning to play an instrument. But then I tell myself I don't have time – an excuse. If the desire is strong enough, I'll give up something less important and use that time. We'll see. I do notice that in the last two books I've written, a character plays the violin. Is my subconscious trying to tell me something?

Step 3

Reengaging With Your Happy, Creative World

Your Creativity and Happiness

Your journey to a happier life began when you read the first word in this book. You decided you want to be a happier person, and you opened up your mind to the idea that you can achieve that goal by being more original. You put two things together, creativity and happiness, and came up with a new idea for your life and attitude.

See how resourceful you are?

Then you relaxed your mind enough to begin reading, listening and understanding. Suddenly you connected with a world that is fluid and rich with creative thoughts and organic joy. Really, don't you feel happier already?

We applaud you for desiring change and wanting to be happy. There really is a glorious, creative world out there, just waiting for you to experience it.

By now, we hope you are not only accepting, but embracing your uniqueness. You don't have to take a vacation or spend one cent to instill joy into your life through creativity. Just look around you, wherever you are. Your environment is a wonderful playground.

The World is Your Playground

Let's think back again to your early life, when you had no trouble tuning-in to the world around you. As we've already discussed, when you were a toddler you probably touched objects within reach, studied them, put them in your mouth to taste. You shook things and listened for sounds, tugged and threw them, not caring about anything except discovery, and asking yourself, "What is this thing and what does it do?"

Everything was new and filled with potential. You even played with your fingers and toes, and all of this exploration and discovery made you happy. The world was your creative playground.

What was happening? Your curiosity prompted you to instinctively engage in your environment and use every one of your senses. You studied your mother's keys, noting the way the silver caught the light. You shook them and heard a jingle. You pressed them to your nose, but there wasn't much of a scent so you put a key in your mouth and felt the ridges with your tongue and tasted the metallic flavor.

These actions were creative and stimulated the sensory pleasure centers of your brain, making you happy. You created a moving, sensual, connected, creative environment that brought you joy.

Additionally, your early creative process involved observing people – the way they talked and dressed, and how they interacted. Then you mimicked what you noticed.

For example, when a little girl gets old enough to

walk, she might put on mommy's high heels and shawl, her pink lipstick, and tromp around imitating what she's observed, pretending to be a grown woman.

Using blocks or cardboard boxes or pieces of wood, youngsters build pretend forts and houses. They draw pictures and cut out snowflakes from construction paper. They dream up detailed stories and play out the parts, becoming cowboys or princesses or dragons.

Jennifer recalls playing alone for hours as a child and being completely content. At five or six years old, she spent a lot of time making up detailed stories complete with characters and plots. She would line up dolls and stuffed animals on the bed and all of them had a part in her little soap opera. Some-times real, live friends would come to the door and ask for her to play outside, but she instructed her mother to tell them she was busy. She didn't want to leave her make-believe world where she was in control of what happened and how the story unfolded. Being the God of her own little world made her happy. Jennifer was connected to her imagination and the joy it produced.

When Mary was a child, she and two of her friends put on roller skating shows in her parents' garage. They spent days planning the show, developing dance numbers, giggling and feeling copious amounts of happiness through wonderful creativity.

You undoubtedly have similar memories of carefree play or make-believe. When you were engaged in those activities, your creative process was at work. You were caught up in the flow of your imagination and you were happy.

Waking Up to the World of Possibilities Around You

As you can see, reengaging with your imagination involves reengaging with your *real* world. That might seem ironic, but in order to reconnect with your imagination, you must be totally present and paying attention to what's around you in reality.

Imaginative ideas are born from truth. We notice something as it is, then ask, *"what if that were this way instead?"* We read real words on a page that bring to life in our minds images, sounds, tastes and personalities. We notice a real problem and create a solution. All of these events involve *paying attention*.

Maybe you're thinking, "But I do pay attention and I'm engaged. Right now, I'm reading and thinking. I go to work, stay late, do housework, cook, talk to my significant other, chase kids or grandkids . . . ."

Those events are all a part of your life, and they offer plenty of opportunities to engage with your imagination; however, the problem is that most of us live our lives on auto-pilot. To really connect with the magnificent world we live in and open up to more creative ideas, you must learn to tune-in to the moment and all it offers. You must start noticing all the elements we take for granted and ignore while in the numbing repetitiveness of our routines.

How many times have you arrived at your place of employment and been unable to remember the details of what you saw during the drive? Or thrown together a quick meal without noticing the texture or subtle aromas of the ingredients? When was the last time you paused a few moments to watch a sunrise or a sunset?

Most people walk through life in a state of semi-hypnosis, unimpressed with colors, shapes, angles, shadows, light, and the other glories of our world. The question is: Why do we do this?

As you learned in Step 1, creative observation and insight tend to decrease as people take on more responsibility, and happiness leaves the building. Also, as we grow older, few of our experiences seem *new* anymore – we've done it all. New *firsts* are scarce.

If you're in this state of bored hypnosis, you've stopped noticing the miraculous in everyday life, and it may seem impossible to you that you'll ever become fascinated with the world around you again. Don't believe it. Like Sleeping Beauty, you can snap out of your trance, and you don't need the Wizard of Oz in order to do so. You already possess the magic.

The Magic of Firsts

In order to recapture the magic, it helps to remember a time when creativity was at work in your life and how it felt.

Try to recall the first time you met someone to whom you felt a strong attraction and write about it in your journal. What physical thing about this person stood out to you most at first sight? Where were you when you first saw this person? Were you at a party? At school? Standing on a street corner? How did you feel? Your heart might have raced at the sight of this person, and you knew you were experiencing something phenomenal.

When remembering, most people think first of a romantic encounter, but parents can also describe the intense magnetism of seeing their child for the first time. As a parent, you probably focused completely on the new addition in your life and the awe, love and sense of protectiveness that swept through you was so immediate and intense it felt all-consuming. Everything about that new being amazed you: tiny fingers and toes, downy skin, the tilt or curve of your baby's nose.

Recall another time in your life when you were amazed at something, as if you were seeing or experiencing it for the first time. It may be something as simple as your first airline flight, or as glorious as your child's first steps.

Step 3 Practice: My Child-like Fascination Experience
In your notebook, answer the following questions about a child-like fascination experience:
1. What was it?
2. Where was I?
3. What was the object or event?
4. How did it make me feel?

Mary's Childlike Fascination Experience
1. **What was it?** Hearing Elvis Presley sing for the first time.
2. **Where was I?** I was in a movie theater with my parents, sister, and aunt and uncle.
3. **What was the object or event?** Elvis was singing

"Love Me Tender."

4. **How did I feel?** I felt as if I were listening to an angel. I'd never heard such a wonderful voice. I began singing along with him and fell into my own little world. I'd never felt such happiness. I was in a mesmerized state of total happiness – Elvis and I singing together.

Jennifer's Childlike Fascination Experience

1. **What was it?** My first trip to New York City in 1994.
2. **Where was I?** Taking a cab ride from the airport to the hotel in Times Square.
3. **What was the object or event?** I was there to attend a writer's conference.
4. **How did I feel?** Exhilarated. Completely alive and aware. Awed by the energy of the city. Fascinated to see so many sights in person that I'd seen all of my life on television and in movies. The cab driver took the scenic route rather than a direct one. We drove through Harlem, and past Central Park. I felt a real sense of excited anticipation at the week ahead, and a real connection to everything around me.

Read what you wrote. The memory of that experience is vivid, isn't it? It stayed with you in vibrant detail. Why? Because you were totally engaged with your world and the event taking place. You were experiencing a first with child-like fascination, which produces the creative flow that we've discussed. The world was your playground.

Whether you were aware of it or not, within this experience you were primed for creativity because child-like fascination is one of the keys to engaging your imagination. And within that realm we find happiness which spills over into our everyday life.

Creating New Firsts

Obviously, most people aren't going to fall in love, have a baby, hear Elvis, or travel to a new city for the first time every day. However, we can still find smaller-scope new firsts to experience each day, or at least once a week, and they can be just as powerful and serve to keep alive that feeling of anticipation, interest, and excitement with life that encourages innovation and happiness.

Start off by challenging yourself to try one new thing per month. Soon, you'll discover you want to do more. Up the challenge to one new thing per week, then one per day. Don't panic. These can be small, easy things:

- Drive a different route to work.
- Take your daily walk in a different neighborhood each day.
- Try a restaurant you've never gone to.
- Sample a food you've never tasted.

Once you're comfortable, try more involved firsts:

- Attempt to start a new friendship by calling up an acquaintance and asking him or her to meet you for coffee.
- Sign up to take a class in a subject that interests

you.
- Rearrange the furniture in your house in an unexpected way.

Of course, you can also attempt the bigger firsts, too:
- Plan a trip to someplace you've never been.
- Face a fear by doing something that frightens you – like public speaking or applying for a new job.

Planning new, long-range events is also a good activity that can bring joy into your life. Jennifer has a long-range goal of visiting every State in the U.S. Just thinking of this goal ignites her imagination with new ideas and possibilities. She also wants to take a class in photography so that she can capture the images of the places she visits.

Mary wants to learn more about astrology, and just recently met a woman who's an astrologer. She made an effort to have coffee with the woman and found that they share much in common.

The idea is to keep life fresh and interesting so that your creativity – and happiness – will flow.

The Sense of Sight – Creative Seeing

While continuing to expose ourselves to new experiences throughout our lives is one key to living creatively and happily, we must also practice seeing *the familiar* with a renewed sense of awestruck wonder. When we mention "seeing," we aren't referring to only the sense of sight. To see creatively, you must be fully present in each moment and experiencing the common objects or events in your life more acutely with *all* of your senses.

For example, the orange you peeled for breakfast – did you pay attention to the nubby texture of the rind against your fingertips? Did you breathe deeply and enjoy the tangy scent and notice the way it made your mouth water? Did you admire the bright orange color and relish the juicy squirt of flavor as you bit into the fruit?

When you stepped outside your house for the first time today, did you sniff the air? While driving to work or running routine errands, did you really look at the homeless man on the corner who's there all of the time, or was he just a passing thought, no more noteworthy than the center stripe on the road?

Next time, really *see* him. What does his body language tell you? Is he beaten down by life and his circumstances, or is he proud and defiant? Beneath the dirt and hair and beard, is he young, middle-aged or old? Can you imagine his life?

Did you notice the grey sparrow outside your window in the early light of dawn this morning? Did you even *acknowledge* the early morning light?

The trick to engaging with your imaginary world is to notice the *ordinary* but in extraordinary ways. Within this fascination time stands still, the pleasure centers of our brains ignite, and joy washes over us.

The way we see the world is a very important factor in the way we create. To see you have to stop *just looking*, the way most people do, and engage your creative mind with your senses. Doing this requires that you look beyond the surface and the obvious, connect and see the unique in the common or familiar.

Everyone sees in different ways. Someone else might look at a girl and see her beautiful blond hair, but you might only see her happy eyes. Seeing is individualized.

For example, as a boy Picasso saw the number 4 and imagined a nose. When Mary sees a 4 she imagines half a tree. When Jennifer looks at a 4 she sees the sail on a sailboat. Other participants in this workshop when looking at a 4 have seen: a pregnant woman, an arrow, and a yoga pose.

What do you see?

When we practice *seeing* as opposed to *just looking,* the familiar becomes new and we experience child-like fascination that ignites our creative minds. And that's when happiness engulfs us. This process is cyclic – the more we "see," the more we are able to imagine, and the more we are able to enjoy our lives.

When you examined the number 4 and visualized it as more than a number, you became more open mentally, and an open mind more readily reacts and deviates from the norm. Deviating from the norm is what creativity is all about.

Also, the more you are able to let go, play, and release preconceived ideas such as, "A 4 is ONLY a 4," the more you will be able to view the world in a fresh way and offer that vision to others. How exciting is that?

Expanding Your Creative Seeing

Let's experience other examples of creative seeing.

Suppose a woman has the creative urge to sew and

decides she is going to learn how. Sewing is a very nice hobby and can be a great business. Additionally, it can be an excellent outlet for creativity. Many women and men have become very happy through sewing and designing clothing.

The creative seeing that takes place in the case of the woman who wants to sew probably began when she viewed something that sparked her interest in the creative skill. She may have spotted a dress she liked but believed she could make it better, prettier, or more stylish. Or she might have seen a piece of fabric that engaged her imagination and she wanted to turn the expensive gabardine into a suit.

It's exactly like when the young Picasso saw a nose instead of a 4, Mary saw a half tree, and Jennifer saw the sail on a sailboat. The woman creatively visualized her own unique version of a piece of clothing and her imagination gave birth to a style all her own.

The Kindle Reader offers us another example of creative seeing. To invent the Kindle, someone had to see a computer shaped as a book. On a simpler scale, the inventor of the sandwich had to see all the foods in a meal combined into one object and eaten without utensils.

When this seeing happens, we experience a rush of creativity and our happiness centers are ignited. Sometimes our vision gives birth to a new object, as in the case of the Kindle and the sandwich. Other times, we simply open our minds to the beauty of the world.

In all of the examples we've mentioned – the new piece of clothing, the sandwich, and the Kindle reader – each idea came to be because the creators were not operating on autopilot as they went about their day. They were fully present in the moment and paying special attention to the sensory details around them. They allowed their minds the flexibility to see beyond the obvious.

Step 3 Practice: Creative Seeing
Let's do a Practice that attempts to reawaken your creative eyes. Study the multiple lines of symbols below. Look beyond the surface. Open your mind and relax.

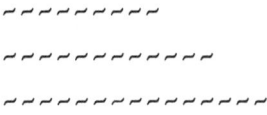

~ ~ ~ ~ ~ ~ ~ ~ ~

~ ~ ~ ~ ~ ~ ~ ~ ~ ~ ~

~ ~ ~ ~ ~ ~ ~ ~ ~ ~ ~ ~ ~

Now, in your notebook, document what you saw.

For right now it doesn't really matter what you saw or didn't see. The point is that you actually tried to see an object actively and didn't just *look*, saying, "They're just grammatical symbols." While seeing, you dropped into your creative space.

If you felt uncomfortable while doing this exercise, that's normal. You're doing something unfamiliar, and people are programmed to perform. Often, we are so steeped in coming up with the right answers to questions or activities that we are totally anxiety-ridden when we are asked to just *see*. And that stress keeps us from opening up to our creative vision, relaxing in our creative space and experiencing happiness.

Take another deep breath and relax before looking again at the line of symbols, and this time make it a game.

See them in ANY way you want. There are no wrong Responses. Let your muscles loosen and know you are going to have fun actively *seeing* rather than passively *looking*.

Now . . . move your eyes back up to the ~~~~~~~

Okay, you're back. Great. What did you see? What was your reaction?

Mary's Responses:
1. **What did you see?** I saw tiny foxes running across the page.
2. **What was your reaction?** Joy. They seem happy.

Jennifer's Responses:
1. **What did you see?** I saw worms crawling across snow.
2. **What was your reaction?** Pleased with myself.

The main point of this short Practice is for you to focus on something, study it in a different way, and acknowledge that you have a certain amount of anxiety when you go to your creative space.

Your Creative World
The more you work to reengage with your creative world by being present in the moment and paying attention, the more active your imaginative world will become. Innovative thoughts will flow through your mind on a daily basis. Creativity will become your routine, and the happiness it brings will be your normal state of being.

In Step 4, we'll move deeper into Practice mode to help you reach this state more quickly and easily.

Creative Happiness Journal Prompt

Write in your journal about your experience with this workshop so far. Here's an idea, if you need one, to help you get started: Writing about what you've learned or experienced while reading Step 3 will really serve to get you ready for the Practices ahead.

Mary's Creative Happiness Journal

It is fun to reengage with my creative world. To take a few moments everyday just to study a sunset or look at the plants in my backyard and envision them as something else – this is what living creatively is all about. Yesterday after working on this chapter, I noticed the morning light and I imagined the shadows as different shapes on the patio.

Also, I saw a rainbow and was delighted with it, which at another time I would have claimed to be too busy to enjoy seeing something like that. That rainbow brought me so much happiness. I actually looked at the colors and noticed how each one slid into the other. Another item I noticed was the inside of a hardboiled egg. I've never seen before how yellow the yoke is.

Writing this book and acknowledging that I have to work with my creativity is making me happier. I feel lighter, brighter and more creative. What a joy to look at a cactus and see a human form in the zig-zag of the plant. I looked at an almond and noticed the ridges and how they look exactly like a Georgia O'Keeffe painting – the running shapes of the New Mexico desert. Life is joyful.

Jennifer's Happiness Creative Journal
While working on this Step with Mary, she mentioned that being present and paying attention doesn't always have to result in a tangible creation in order to bring happiness. Sometimes our minds are simply opened to the beauty of the world and we are able to experience that beauty in new ways, or as if we're seeing it for the first time.

I recall one such moment in my life. I was driving with my husband to our cabin in Colorado one day in September. We've made that drive so often over the years that it has become routine and I take it for granted. I usually sit in the passenger seat and read while my husband drives. For some reason, on this particular day I closed my book and really saw the scenery around me. I tuned in to what was outside my window, the experience I was having, and my reaction to it. The way the aspen leaves flickered in the sunlight and the gravel road unfurled like a curved ribbon through the forest ahead of us. The jostling motion of the truck, the hum of the engine, the buffeting sound of the wind at the windows. Suddenly I felt a part of it all, connected to the trees, the sunlight, the wind, and that time with my husband in the truck. The moment was mine, and I remember thinking that I was experiencing pure happiness. The rest of the world fell away and I was fully present in the experience and the place. I felt like I was driving through those woods for the first time and seeing them with new eyes. I wanted to freeze that instant in time, and in essence, I did. I can close my eyes and relive it instantly. My imagination recreates it at will. So I suppose I did create something. I created a vivid memory.

Step 4

Deepening Your Creative Happiness

More Ways to Break Out of The Routine Trap

As you've learned from the previous Steps, when you become too familiar with your environment, you aren't as creative as you're capable of being. Routine can sap creative energy. So let's move deeper now into your sensory world.

Even if you aren't totally unhappy with your routine and life, the thrill of being alive and seeing the world differently may have lessened for you. When this happens, your pleasure center snuffs out and life is blah. When boredom becomes too much, some people even search for unsafe ways to reignite it, making life dangerous.

We aren't insinuating that you should throw out your schedule for the sake of creativity and/or happiness. That would just make you crazy. However, we want to show you how to use your mind to shift your perspective for just five minutes a day while you are in the midst of your routine for more creativity and happiness.

Also, you can carry this new perspective over into whatever creative outlets you're exploring. Whether it's photography, decorating, cooking, writing, painting or something else, the world-perception enhancing Practices in this Step will enrich any creative activity.

Your Perspective Toy Box

Learn to use your perspective toy box to awaken to the many glorious creative encounters available to you. This imaginary box is filled with similes, metaphors and synesthesia techniques that will shift your viewpoint into a more creative mode and help you experience the world more fully.

To start, let's pull metaphors and similes from our perspective toy boxes and examine them. Then we'll practice.

The Magnificent Metaphor and Sensational Simile

If the mere mention of metaphors and similes throws you back in time to eighth grade English and makes you break out in a cold sweat, relax. We're going to make this easy and fun, even if English was never your thing and you never quite grasped the concept of metaphors and similes.

Simply put, a metaphor states that something *is* something else. Here's an example: *My love is a red rose.*

Of course, we all know love *isn't* a red rose. However when you see red roses you sometimes think of love, right? They've become a symbol of romance.

Similes are like metaphors, except rather than saying something *is* something else, they only make a comparison, often by using the word '**like**'. For example here's the metaphor we just mentioned turned into a simile: *My love is like a red rose.*

A simile is metaphor-lite!

The parallels of red roses and love are clear if you think about it. Like a red rose, love is beautiful, soft and delicate. But it can be thorny and painful, too. Either way, it affects our hearts. And, of course, hearts are red.

Here's a quick, easy exercise to clarify metaphors and similes even more and help you create one of your own in a few, happy seconds.

In your journal, do the following in simile form:
Describe your love life:
My love life is like . . .

You might've stated that your love life is like a hurricane or a storm or a warm pool of water. Or perhaps you said, "I don't have a love life, so I suppose it's like a desert!"

People think in metaphors and similes all of the time, we just don't notice it. For instance, you might think, "Gosh, the kitchen looks like a hurricane hit it." (Simile) This sort of comparison helps us to understand the world around us and explain it to others. A person might be confused about her love life and can't figure out what's wrong, but by shifting her perspective and turning her love life into a simile or metaphor, she might gain a better understanding of the dynamic of it. And understanding brings relief and happiness.

Step 4 Practice: Easy Similes and Metaphors
In your journal, complete the following:
1. My feet are(metaphor)
2. My closet is/looks like(simile)

3. My family members on holidays are like (simile)
4. Anger is(metaphor)

Mary's Responses:
1. My feet are paddles for the sidewalk.
2. My closet looks like K-mart after a dollar special.
3. My family members on holidays are like monkeys in the zoo.
4. Anger is hot and red.

Jennifer's Responses:
1. My feet are blocks of ice.
2. My closet looks like a denim outlet store.
3. My family members on holidays are like stuffed turkeys.
4. Anger is a festering wound.

While you are stuck in traffic or standing in line at the supermarket, look around and practice developing similes and metaphors. You might ask yourself:
1. What or who does the woman or man standing next to me resemble?
2. What does the car in front of me look like?
3. What is that cloud similar to in appearance?
4. What do the kids on the street corner sound like?

Step 4 Practice: The Egg and I
This Practice requires an egg. If you don't have eggs handy, close your eyes and imagine one. Think of the many ways in which eggs can be cooked and how they

appear afterward, such as: hard boiled, poached, over easy, over medium, over hard, scrambled, made into an omelet, microwaved.

Now imagine yourself as an egg. Weird, I know, but let go and have fun. What kind of egg best defines you? Use your new simile/metaphor technique to describe yourself, and then note in your journal why that description fits.

I am a/an _____egg because...

Jennifer's Responses
I am a scrambled egg because my mind is always scattered in ten different directions at once.

Mary's Responses
I'm a soft-boiled egg because I'm hard on the outside, mush on the inside.

Adding Your Senses To Metaphors and Similes
Maybe you haven't noticed, but people often combine the senses with metaphors and similes. For example when we say, "She's as sweet as pie," we are using the sense of taste to describe a person's disposition. When we say, "He has a hot temper," we are using the sense of touch to describe a personality trait. And when we say, "Wow, that red and orange striped dress screams, 'notice me!'" we are using our sense of sound to describe the appearance of an object.

Sensory descriptors spice up our language and get our point across in more interesting and creative ways.

Step 4 Practice: What Is Love?

Let's practice using sensory details in imaginative ways that breathe life into our descriptions. Allow yourself to think freely and take chances with this Practice. Remember, you can't be wrong, and no answer is stupid.

Let your mind wander into silly territory. Not everything in life has to be serious and correct.

First, think for a moment about love (not sex – you can do that later.) What is it like to love someone? Since your feelings of love for one person can be quite different in nature to your feelings of love for another person, it might help to focus on your relationship with one person in particular. Or perhaps even your love for a pet.

When you have someone or something in mind, answer the following questions:

1. What does love look like?
2. What does love taste like?
3. What does love sound like?
4. What does love feel like?
5. What does love smell like?

Great, you're finished. Pat yourself on the back. The above Practice isn't easy because it maximizes your creative thought. If you struggled a bit and would like to try again, read over our Responses then give it another shot.

Mary's similes about love:
1. Love looks like cotton candy, spun into pink gold.
2. Love tastes like chocolate sunshine.
3. Love sounds like Frank Sinatra on his best day.

4. Love feels like the softest robe in the world after a warm bath
5. Love smells like Opium perfume, confident, strong and romantic.

Jennifer's similes about love:
1. Love looks like a pomegranate – blood red and perfect, despite the bumps.
2. Love tastes like the first sip from a hot cup – delicious, but you never know when it might burn you.
3. Love sounds like soft rain, washing away the heartache and making everything fresh and new again.
4. Love feels like the first day of school – exciting, fearful and hopeful, filled with promise and possibility.
5. Love smells like coffee – rich and full and lingering.

Step 4 Practice: Pepper Upper
You'll need pepper for the next Practice. Find some in your spice cabinet, borrow from a neighbor, or head to the store. We'll wait.

Okay, now that you have your pepper, pour a small amount of it into your hand and examine it carefully, then jot down what the pepper looks like in simile form.

Jennifer's Response:
Pepper looks like ashes.

Mary's Response:
Pepper looks like miles of exotic volcanic sand. The mound of pepper also reminds me of tiny bits of tan and black fabric cut up into confetti. For the first time, I noticed that pepper isn't all black – it's also tan. Amazing!

If you aren't allergic to pepper, put a tiny amount of it on your tongue then complete the following statement:
Pepper tastes like . . .

Jennifer's Response:
Pepper tastes like smoke.

Mary's Response:
Pepper tastes like gun powder banging around in my mouth.

Now take a pinch of pepper and rub it between two fingers. Complete this sentence:
Pepper feels like . . .

Jennifer's Response:
Pepper feels like a back scratch.

Mary's Response:
Pepper feels like carpet beneath my feet.

The next statement for you to complete about pepper requires you to reach far into your creative "perspective" tool box and make a slightly offbeat kind of connection.

As the cliché says, "open your mind and think outside the box." Finish this sentence:

Pepper sounds like . . .

Was that more difficult? For many people not used to this sort of creative comparison, it is, so don't feel alone if you couldn't come up with an answer right away.

We know that pepper doesn't make a sound, but what if it did? Stretch your mental muscles and ask yourself what pepper would sound like if it *could* make noise.

Mary's Response: Pepper sounds like firecrackers, explosions bright with blue.

Jennifer's Response: Pepper sounds like a crackling fire.

The above Practice can be done using all types of different foods or objects. For example answer the same questions using salt, sugar, a pebble, a twig, or a favorite old shoe.

Synesthesia

In the last Practice, when you described what pepper sounds like you used a technique called synesthesia, which literally means to "exchange the senses."

As we've already noted, on its own pepper doesn't actually have a sound. We can look at pepper, taste it, feel it, but we can't really hear it. So when you described pepper as having a sound, you creatively exchanged one or more senses for another. In other words, you considered the more obvious traits of pepper – its appearance, smell, taste and texture – and used those to imagine what *sound* pepper would make if it could.

The creative technique of synesthesia uses one sense, such as sound, to describe something that is usually described with another sense, such as sight. Here are a few more simple examples of synesthesia:

A Loud shirt: A shirt has no sound, but it can "look loud" if the color is bold and bright or the fabric's pattern is chaotic.

Bitter wind: We can't really taste the wind, but it can feel bitter if it is harsh and unrelenting.

Wine connoisseurs use synesthesia when they review chardonnays, pinots and other wines by describing the taste as "green," "crisp," "velvety," or "breezy." We know wine can't taste crisp or velvety, which are touch words not taste; however, we always get the picture with synesthesia. Wine that has a tangy taste, like a green apple, might be described as "crisp." Wine with a chocolate taste might be described as "smooth," "rich" or "velvety," all words that are associated with chocolate.

Step 4 Practice: Sip It

Let's have some more fun using synesthesia. Pour yourself a small glass of wine, water, cola, tea or juice. Take a sip of your drink then using three different *sight* words (words that typically describe something you can see) describe the taste.

1. This drink tastes like . . .

2. This drink tastes like . . .
3. This drink tastes like . . .

Mary's Responses
1. This wine tastes like yellow and white daisies in summer.
2. This wine tastes like foggy mist.
3. This wine tastes like velvet sprinkled with diamonds.

Jennifer's Responses
1. This water tastes like a blue sky.
2. This water tastes like sparkling snow.
3. This water tastes like sunshine.

Practice creating one simile or metaphor each day using synesthesia, maybe as you're brushing your teeth or cooking dinner. As you practice, the process will get easier, and suddenly you will notice how the world is turning into a fine wine, and your life is a bed of roses.

Creative Happiness Journal Prompt
Write in your journal about your thoughts regarding your journey with this workshop so far. Here's a prompt if you need an idea to guide you: Write about your experience with similes, metaphors, synesthesia and your creativity.

Jennifer's Creative Happiness Journal
I love experimenting with the techniques in this Step. When I teach classes or give workshops on creativity, I

always have the students or participants engage in many exercises like this. They are usually amazed at the responses they and others come up with, and they have a lot of fun. Another exercise I often use involves smell. I bring plastic bags filled with cotton balls soaked in different scents then divide everyone into groups. Each group gets one bag and each bag contains a different scent. The group has to write a description of the scent using non-scent-related words. They read their description aloud and everyone else in the other groups has to guess what the scent is. Sometimes the people writing the description aren't sure themselves. This is great, because they have to rely strictly on what their nose is telling them.

Scent is such a powerful sense. The smell of Jergen's lotion takes me back to visits to my grandmother's house. She always wore Jergen's and its smell brings back so much, even other senses. My grandmother's softness and the warmth of her smile, the songs she hummed while she washed dishes or cooked, the taste of ice cold Dr. Pepper in a glass bottle. One sniff and I recall the carefree feelings associated with childhood summers, a sense of safety and security and love. I see the yellow flash of fireflies in the grass on sultry Texas nights, feel the smooth, cool rind of a slice of watermelon and see the seed-speckled, juicy red fruit. I hear my cousins' laughter as we twirl on swings in the park. I could go on. Recreating these memories so vividly makes the life I'm living now so much richer and gives me a real sense of satisfaction.

Mary's Creative Happiness Journal

As an author, I adore similes, metaphors and synesthesia techniques. They are the mark of a very creative person/ writer. Plus they are a heck of a lot of fun. Within the classroom or workshop, I'm always amazed at how creative each person is when encouraged. And I have never failed to learn through the metaphors and similes that my students create. Now that is a gift. The more I work with these techniques the more my creativity develops.

When reading, if I read a perfect simile or metaphor and note the use of synesthesia, I'm entranced with the writer. F. Scott Fitzgerald and his novel *The Great Gatsby* is a master with similes and metaphors. His pastoral references are joyful. I never tire of studying his creativity in the perfect American novel that he wrote years ago – it's fresh, unique and inspiring every time I read it.

Step 5

Group Creativity

Why Share Your Creativity with Another Person?
Creative people are often stereotyped as solitary souls who suffer in life, crave isolation, and are only highly inventive when they are alone.

This is simply *not true.* The two of us met at a creative writing group conference and have benefitted from our participation with one another over the years.

Most creative individuals find that they are more inspired and happy when they interact with others who share their interests and relate to their struggles and desires. In fact, studies on the subject indicate that complete creative gratification *requires* social interaction. For example, interpersonal support may be important during the creative process, and an audience is necessary after a project is completed in order for the creator to feel fulfilled.

Participating in a positive and balanced creativity group can be encouraging, help you commit to your activities of self-expression, and increase your overall happiness.

Everyone Needs an Audience

Imagine for a moment a group of cave people highlighted in firelight, watching a woman scratch images onto a cave wall. When she finishes, the woman joins her friends around the fire and begins to tell an amazing story, her face enhanced by the flickering amber light as she gestures at her artwork.

Her audience smiles and nods, their eyes wide and curious. They are inspired and intrigued by the woman's words and pictures. And the woman, encouraged by their responses, feels proud of her work.

What was taking place in that cave? The woman was sharing her way of seeing life and the world with her peers for their consideration and enjoyment. Since the beginning of time, creative people have sought out an audience, and we're no different today. We need to share our creations with someone and have our work acknowledged in order to feel as if it's worthwhile. It's as simple as that.

An age-old question is applicable here: *If a tree falls in the forest and no one hears it, is there still a sound?*

Innovators need someone to acknowledge their work in order to feel as if it even exists outside of their own private world. The responses of others bring value to your mode of self-expression, be it photography, writing, painting, scrapbooking, or baking.

If you don't reveal your creative projects to others, part of your creative identity will be lost. Of course, you might feel vulnerable sharing at first. It can be frightening and intimidating to expose your efforts to another person. However, once you get past the fear, great pride and happiness is your reward. And the more you share, the more innovative you will become and the happier you will be as you begin to recognize the validity and importance of your unique mode of self-expression.

Positive Audiences Equal Support for Creatives

When you find a positive audience for your creativity, you've found a foundation of emotional support. A group or even just one person who understands creativity and how important it is can be a great source of inspiration, encouragement, energy and validation.

Remember when you were a child and you made something then showed it to someone? You may have run home from school or skipped out of your bedroom to show your mother or father what you had done. When they praised and encouraged you, you felt proud and creative.

You still need that praise and encouragement, perhaps even more than you did as a child. Children haven't had time to develop many self-doubts. You, on the other hand, have dealt with rejections and disappointments that are a normal part of life. Even though they're common to everyone, that accumulation of rejections and fears can whittle away at your creative self-confidence, little by little.

When you create exclusively in isolation, you miss out on receiving the dynamic inspiration that comes from connecting with other people and soaking in their reactions, opinions, and ideas. This isn't one-sided; when people share their creations with you, the same benefits occur. Your own imagination kicks into gear.

Also, as a member of an audience you learn that others have doubts similar to yours. A supportive group may say to you, "You shouldn't feel badly because I've had similar experiences, problems or heartache." Humans thrive knowing we are in that same boat.

Step 5 Practice: Show and Tell
Let's try an exercise that will help you realize more clearly how beneficial sharing your creative pursuits with others can be. Recall a time when you created something, shared it with another person and had a positive experience. This event can be recent or when you were a child. Write about it in in your journal using the following prompt:

When I was
I made/created/thought up a/an
and shared it with
After sharing my I felt because . . .

Mary's Responses
When I was fifty
I made a painting of fish
and shared it with other art class members.
After sharing my painting, I felt proud because I had taken a chance and painted, and the people I showed it to said it was pretty.

Jennifer's Responses

When I was in my thirties
I wrote a short story in a creative writing class
and shared it with the students and teacher by reading
it aloud. Afterward, I felt nervous but energized and
eager to write more stories because I was given both
encouragement and constructive criticism I could use
to make my writing better.

Realizing you had a positive experience of sharing your
creation helps you understand more fully that communion
with other encouraging, supportive people is important.
It builds happiness and self-esteem that stimulates even
more innovative ideas in your mind. Also, sharing helps
us become less inhibited and take more risks, lifting our
creativity to an even higher level.

Inspiration and Supportive Creative Groups

It's fun to brainstorm or talk about projects or creativity
in general, even more so when you've found a group or a
creative partner with an understanding of what you are
doing and a mutual interest in helping one another.

Also, when you are in tune with other creative spirits
you understand your creative problems more fully. As
Clark Moustakas, Humanistic psychologist, states about
creativity, "Realization of one's uniqueness is felt . . . in
moments of communion with others."

What You Need From a Creative Group or Partner

While becoming involved with creative groups or teaming

up with another person can be very beneficial, you must make a conscious effort to find the *right* group or partner. This person or persons should be positive and upbeat so you will reflect that constructive attitude.

When seeking a group or partner, look for a spirit of optimism, encouragement and constructive help. If these qualities are missing, don't join. If you already have joined this type of group, leave and do NOT go back.

Why?

Because your creativity is like your baby. You wouldn't willingly expose your child to a negative and potentially dangerous situation, would you? Interacting and sharing your ideas with negative people sucks the creative energy right out of you, taking your happiness with it.

So how can you be sure if a particular partner or group is right for you? Ask yourself if they offer you the following four components:

Active Audience

When you share your ideas or something you've created, a good audience will take an active interest. They don't repeatedly interrupt to talk about unrelated topics, text, or engage in other distractions.

Safe Environment

When you are with your group or partner you should feel you are in a safe environment. If you feel that your ideas are attacked or not heard, the environment isn't a positive one, so it isn't safe. Such slights might not be blatant – they might simply come to you through your intuitive feelings. DO NOT try to silence or disregard your intuition. It will tell you if something is wrong and you should beware. Run, don't walk, away from this group or person.

Empathy

The right person or group will show empathy for your creative struggles. As creatives, we all face difficulties. Understanding from a sympathetic person or persons who realize what you're going through can help immensely in working through anxiety and bolstering self-confidence. A good group or partner will commiserate and lift you up.

Give and Take

The most beneficial groups or partners give equal time to all parties involved. Each person is allowed the opportunity to share, and during that time that individual is the focus of all encouragement, brainstorming effort and discussion. Of course, circumstances may dictate that on certain occasions one member requires more attention than the others. However, one particular person dominating *every* meeting should not become the norm. There should be a sense of balance within the group.

As you can see, all of the above add up to *support*. Simply put, the right partner or group will support you and your creative endeavors.

For example, when Mary was learning to write novels she joined a small writers' group that taught her about publishing, format, and technique. It would have taken her years to learn what she did in a few short months with this group. She also enjoyed a great deal of emotional support from the group whenever she received rejection letters from publishers, because the other group members had also received rejections and understood the emotional turmoil she was experiencing.

If you are in the right group or with the right creative partner, you will realize it in the first few weeks. If there is any type of negative energy, get out of the group or break off from the person immediately. This type of situation will not change for the better; it will only get worse. Do not try to fix it.

You should feel trust and be comfortable. With each meeting you should grow more confident. For example, your group may help you break through creative blocks by cutting through confusion. When someone values and supports your vision, that positivity manifests into more creative energy for you.

What You DON'T Need From a Creative Group

You do not need negative criticism from your group or partner because this type of criticism can impede your creativity. Attaching disapproval to a vision is the fastest way to inhibit it. Are you willing to become fodder for people to vent their creative hostilities? We hope not. If you sense this sort of tension between members in a group – or if only one member possesses this tension – run! No good can come to you from being in such a group.

If you decide to join a group that offers critique to

its members, make sure that the criticisms made are constructive and given in the spirit of helpfulness, brainstorming, and discussion. If given and received in this manner, constructive criticism can help you take your project or idea to a new level.

The trick is to know yourself and trust your intuition. If you are overly-sensitive and you know you are likely to become defensive, even over criticism that is delivered in the spirit of helpfulness and in a kind way, don't join this type of group or partnership.

If, on the other hand, you welcome commentary, make certain to only take the suggestions that instinctively feel right and leave the others behind. Practice saying, "Thanks, I'll take that into consideration," and leave it at that.

Another element you don't want or need in a group or partnership is competition between members. For example, if you have decided to take photographs and you join a photography club, make sure when members share photos there is not a sense of trying to one-up each other. Everyone's creativity should be valued in and of itself. There is no better, just different. And different is what makes us unique.

Don't join a group or partnership without at least a few rules. However, make sure the rules aren't so inflexible that the atmosphere feels like a police state.

Jennifer joined and left several critique groups over a period of years before she found the one that fit. She isn't comfortable with rigid structure, so groups that are so bound by procedures that they have a written rulebook were not for her. She found that those types of groups always seemed to have one person in charge – or who thought she was. The restrictions made it difficult to relax and let creative interaction flow between members.

However, Jennifer also discovered that a total lack of structure and protocol in a group could cause problems because certain members have one set of expectations, while others have another. This caused a real problem in one of her groups when one member quit bringing anything to share and another member confronted her about it, saying she would have to leave the group if she didn't start producing.

In the end, the group fell apart because it became apparent that different members wanted different things from the interaction.

Know what you are getting into from the beginning. If you are considering joining an already formed group, ask about the ways in which they conduct their meetings, what is expected, and if there are rules.

If you are starting a new group from scratch, spend some time discussing the needs and expectations of each member in the partnership before getting started. You will quickly get a sense of whether or not the group is a fit for you by noting if the other members are seeking the same type of collaboration that you are.

The Road to Constructive Criticism
Let's delve a little deeper into constructive criticism. Creative groups that meet for constructive criticism tend to operate best when the group members know each other

well enough to completely relax and trust one another. This type of relationship and trust takes time to build, so if you're starting a new group, strive to bring together members who already share this bond.

Alternately, if you are considering joining an already formed group that offers critique, then visit and ONLY LISTEN for several meetings. DO NOT submit your creative projects or ideas right away. Make sure you trust the individual(s) first and feel relaxed and supported while with them.

When you begin to critique with a group or another person, the relationship is complicated and could possibly become more complicated as time goes on. You need to always be aware of this. Conflicts may occur because feelings get hurt over the criticism, bent rules, or any other number of perceived problems. (Note Jennifer's experience above).

You may end up giving more critique or receiving too much. And you must realize that some people do not know how to give constructive criticism, and sadly may not have your best interest at heart.

Also some people feel powerful when criticizing others. Mary was once in a creative writing critique group with four other women. The group only lasted six months because the members' feelings were hurt by critiques that were done in a vendetta-like way. Also, over time, the women who got publishing contracts were targets for jealousy from the others who were not published. The group became a detriment to Mary's creative spirit and she left the group before her creative spirit was irrevocably harmed.

Don't stop searching out or attempting to create a group that's a good fit for you. Jennifer's current group evolved over time into the strong and unified gathering of members it is today. Early on, people left the group who weren't getting what they wanted from it. When they did, the remaining members were careful about letting anyone in who didn't come with the highest recommendation from one of the other people in the group. Jennifer now enjoys and benefits her interaction with a group of mature, easy-going, innovative women who are all committed to a similar vision – that of helping one another achieve their creative dreams.

Step 5 Practice: Realization Exercise
Recall a time when you shared your creativity with a person or a group and you experienced negative feedback. This might've occurred when you were a child, or just yesterday. Now, answer the following questions in your journal:

> When I was(age)
> I made/created/thought up a/an
> and shared it with
> After sharing my
> I felt because

Mary's Responses
> When I was 25
> I created a novel

and shared it with my ex-husband.
After sharing my novel I felt devastated because
he told me I couldn't write (ergo that is why he is my
ex-husband!)

Jennifer's Responses
When I was a newlywed,
I made a pot roast for the first time, adding my own
extra dash of certain ingredients that I thought would
enhance the flavor. After serving it to my husband,
he told me that from now on we should just eat my
mother's pot roast when visiting her. I felt disappointed,
but also a little amused. (Because he was right; the pot
roast was terrible!) I also felt as if I was a failure as a
cook, and to this day I consider myself to be only an
average cook and don't risk trying to make anything
that's too complicated.

Do you see how a negative experience can affect a
person and be a detriment to their creativity? Starting
today, don't let negative reactions to your creativity keep
you from being innovative, taking creative risks, and
being happy.

The journey of creativity is not about good or bad, it
is about feeling happy, joyful and fulfilled. And bonding
with another creative person or group, can be the very
essence of happiness.

**Step 5 Practices: Finding and/or Bonding with Other
Creatives**

Make a List

Make a list of creative people with whom you feel comfortable. This might be one person or ten. When your list is complete, call each person and discuss the possibility of forming a creative group.

Make the Rules

Think about what you want out of a group or partnership and have all other potential members do the same. Write these down and make sure each item on the list strives to serve not only the group as a whole, but each potential member's creativity. Rules on this list might include:

- We won't take ourselves too seriously.
- There will be no negative criticism.
- Our ultimate goals are enjoyment and inspiration.
- Time will be set aside for each person to share.

Have a meeting to discuss everyone's list of "rules" and come up with a final list.

Visit A Group

Visit an already functioning creativity group, such as a photography club, quilting circle, painting or writing club. Introduce yourself and then actively listen. Take note of different aspects and dynamics within the group. For example:

- Do group members look happy/sad/

anxious?
- Do all/some/few group members participate?
- Is the overall atmosphere surrounding the group happy/stressful/distant?

Use the above notes to help you decide whether or not you should become a member of the group. Concerning your creativity and happiness, this may be the most important decision you will make.

You've Found a Group or Creative Person. What Now?
The following are ideas for activities you might choose to explore in your new group.

Surprise and Creativity
Write down what surprises you about life then share it with your group or a trusted creative friend, and listen to their surprises. Be sure to express positive feedback.

Inquiring Minds Want to Know
Choose three of your favorite Practices from this book and ask group members to answer them orally. Then give positive feedback. It's also a good idea to have your group work through this book together and share all your Responses.

Brainstorming Creatively
Brainstorm with your group or creative friend about new projects. Listen to all ideas even if ideas

don't feel right to you. Practice giving positive feedback.

Getting To Know You

Ask the following questions of group members or creative people and share your Responses with them:

- When did you first realize that creativity made you happy?
- What do you do when you are blocked creatively?
- How do you keep your creative energy high?
- What is the most important component of your creativity?
- How are you inspired?

Creative Happiness Journal Prompt

Write in your journal about your thoughts regarding your journey with this workshop so far. Here's a prompt if you need an idea to guide you: Write about your thoughts or experiences of sharing your creativity and belonging to a group. You might comment on how you feel in groups and how joining a creative support group might be beneficial.

Mary's Creative Happiness Journal

I have a major love-hate relationship with creative groups. Most of the groups with which I've been associated have been creative writing groups where the emphasis was on criticism. As a writer I was ready for the criticism, but as a researcher and instructor I observed how critique groups can make people unhappy. I finally bowed out of all critique groups, found individual writers that I trusted to critique my writing, and moved on from there.

However, I missed the communion with other imaginative people. I craved being with creatives and rejoicing in the creative act. With this in mind, ten years ago I started a group with two other women just to enjoy our creativity. Both women were published writers and loved to write. We started out with rules: no critique, writing for the enjoyment of writing, and talking about writing in a positive way. Those were the guiding posts for the group's success. We met for three years until I moved from Texas to Nevada.

We were so happy, and all of us experienced exponential growth in our writing abilities. We loved each other, held sacred each of our creative spirits and rejoiced in the fact we could just acknowledge each other's creations and feel happy. The formula worked well because, after participating in that group for a year, I wrote my three best books: *What To Keep, The Lighthouse,* and *Falling Out of Bed.*

Now I teach creative writing, and supporting writers is what I do best and is my biggest goal. Writers come to me who are so beaten down from being in critique groups that they can't write. I creatively coach writers who have been told they can't write. How do I do this? I take a deep breath and say, "Baby, you can write. You've just lost your creative spirit and I'm going to help you find it again."

Jennifer's Creative Happiness Journal

As a writer, I honestly don't know what I would do without my writing critique group. We meet every Wednesday night at my house and read our work to one another. We bring a copy for each person to follow along and mark on as the reading proceeds. We're a pretty loosely structured group. This works best for me because I feel stifled by too many rules. However, our loose structure only works because we've managed to join together a group of five mature people who respect one another, and that results in everything falling naturally into place.

At the beginning of each meeting – or by email before we meet – we take a head count of who is reading that night and how much they have to read. If too many people are reading too many pages, making for a very late night, the person or persons not on deadline typically offer to go last, and only if it isn't past a certain time by then. It's a very agreeable, workable method. As for criticism, the respect factor comes into play there, as well.

Our purpose is to help, encourage and support one another, however we also want to challenge each other to grow and reach our respective goals. All criticism is delivered in a constructive way, not a mean way. In fact, I hesitate to call it criticism. It is more in the form of suggestions or opinions. We call it brainstorming and we all get involved.

I am secure enough that if one of the members offers an idea/suggestion/or opinion that doesn't feel right to me for my work, I just thank them for it and let it go. They do the same. None of us are there for some sort of warped power fix. We are all there to make our respective writing stronger. And I find that often, even if I don't agree with an idea that's offered, it still triggers something in my mind that helps me to go off in a new direction where I *do* find the right fix for my story.

Everyone responds differently to certain kinds of groups. I think that if a person wants to be a member of a creative group, the key is to try on different types of groups for size until you find the right fit.

Step 6

Conquering Creative Challenges

Creative Atmosphere

People who make creativity an important, routine part of their lives have learned to manipulate the atmosphere around them in a way that nurtures their powers of invention.

For example, we are always meeting people who say to us, "I'd like to write a book, but I don't have the time." We usually just smile politely and bite our tongues rather than explain that we, too, had a full plate of obligations when we started writing, and we still do, however, we have always found the time to write.

When Jennifer was writing and trying to sell her first novel, she had a part-time job as an office manager at a law firm, a residential rental property business she ran with her husband, was raising two active boys, and volunteered as PTA treasurer at their elementary school.

"I thought I didn't have time to write, but then I realized plenty of other busy mothers with jobs wrote books, and I had the same 24 hours in my day as they did in theirs," she says.

So Jennifer started making *better use of her time.* She got up an hour earlier in the morning to write. She gave up a few television programs she didn't really care about watching. She made use of the minutes she spent waiting in the car to pick up her sons from sports practices and other after-school activities by writing in a notebook she kept in her purse.

When Mary began writing her first novel, she was working on a Masters degree, teaching, and raising an active teenager. She used the slash and burn method for creating more time. She quit doing "lunches," screened phone calls, began shopping from catalogs, and got up hours earlier to write. These adjustments provided her an extra three hours a day to write.

As you can see, we both manipulated our atmosphere and did not make excuses about why we couldn't write. You can do the same for your creative endeavor. By 'atmosphere' we mean:

- Time to create
- Physical space to create in
- Emotional support from loved ones and friends
- Financial freedom to create

It's time for you to think hard, be honest, and admit the excuses you make to NOT create. These are your creative challenges and are usually connected to some part of your atmosphere. Right now ask yourself what is keeping you from devoting yourself to exploring your creativity and bringing more joy into your life. In your journal, list the following:

My excuse(s):

Now, think about possible ways you might solve this problem(s) and fulfill your creative need(s). Write your ideas, no matter how silly they seem, in your journal.

If your list makes your heart sink because you think you'll never overcome these creative challenges, relax. The truth is, it doesn't matter how much time you think you have, or if you have a comfortable, inspiring room in which to create, supportive friends and family, or financial freedom. We are going to help you realize that you have the time, room, emotional support, and the financial means to create.

Time to Create

You might believe time is your biggest challenge, and it is a very real one, but don't fall into the trap of thinking your life will fall apart if you give up a few of your current activities and use the extra time for your creative interests.

Right now, in your journal, list all the events that typically fill your days. Prioritize, then make a pact with yourself to cut at least one time waster out of your life this week, and use the extra time for your creativity. The "time waster" could be shopping, talking on the telephone, or watching some mindless TV programs.

Physical Space

What if your biggest issue is space rather than time? Maybe you live in an apartment or a small house and there's not a room you can claim for your creativity. Or if you do have a room, perhaps it's windowless or used for storage and the surroundings are far from mentally stimulating.

Excuses, excuses, excuses.

We know of a woman who converted a closet into her writing space. Since there was no window, for a view she cut out inspiring photographs from magazines and taped them to the walls. Mary writes in the library, while Jennifer has found a space at a coffee shop.

Jennifer's husband, whose creative outlet is woodworking, was limited to what he could do in their cramped garage and he decided he needed a shop. But the City wouldn't allow him to build an enclosed structure in their backyard because of fire restrictions. So he had a concrete slab poured, put up a carport, and now works beneath it, using tarps to cover his equipment and protect them from the weather. In the colder months, he uses an outdoor heater. Instead of giving up or making excuses, he manipulated his environment in a way that allows him the space he needs to pursue his creative passion.

In your journal, note where you create and how you can make your space better.

Emotional Support from Loved Ones

Maybe you have a great space and plenty of time but no emotional support or encouragement from your family and friends. They might think you're wasting your time or consider your new activity an imposition or even a threat to their relationship with you. Or maybe they are jealous.

First, tell them calmly how important creating is to you, how it nurtures your happiness, and how the time you spend on it will make you a better wife, mother, daughter, sister and/or friend.

Don't expect an overnight change in attitude. Instead, seek other people who share your interest who will give you emotional support, and form a weekly or monthly group (see Step 5). Or at least schedule a routine phone call to a like-minded person to share the joys you both experience through creativity.

Financial Freedom to Create

For many people, the greatest excuse and need is money – funds for creative supplies or the required fees for seminars, workshops or conferences that can be great sources of creative knowledge and inspiration.

If you're faced with the money problem, think about starting a creativity fund. This fund can be as rudimentary as a jelly jar on your bedside table. At the end of each day, transfer the spare change in your pockets or purse into the jar. Then use your imagination to come up with ways to earn extra cash to add to the fund.

Investigate avenues that will allow you to attend functions free-of-charge. Often, volunteering your time at a seminar will earn you a free or discounted ticket. And many seminars and conferences offer scholarships. If you find one, apply.

Additionally, figure out how you can cut back on what you believe are essentials. Do you really need twelve designer handbags, fake nails, an expensive phone, eight magazine subscriptions you don't read, a new truck, or full cable?

When Mary began writing, she decided to simplify her life so she'd have more time and money to devote to the endeavor. She grew her hair out to shoulder length, had it blunt cut and began wearing it fashionably pulled back. She saved thousands of dollars on haircuts. She saved time, too. She began doing her own nails, bought cosmetics at the pharmacy instead of a high-end department store, and gave up expensive lattes.

The old cliché, "Where there's a will, there's a way," is true. A little ingenuity will help you find solutions to your greatest needs, giving you the power to break through any roadblock – real or perceived – that's keeping you from following your imagination in the direction it is trying to lead you.

In your journal, list where you can cut back and use the extra money and/or time for your creativity.

Creativity Fear

What if you've identified your needs, taken care of them, but still find yourself making excuses for why you "can't" create? Your excuses offer clues to your fears about creating.

Right now in your journal, write down your biggest fear about creating.

Understand that it's not unusual for people to be afraid to try something new, especially if it has to do with creativity. Unfortunately, no magic pill exists that will banish your fears about creating; however, you can learn to look past your fears and find creative happiness if you're willing to take a risk so that you can reach your full potential.

To end a creative fear, keep creating and "break through" your fear. Jennifer can attest to this method. One of her biggest fears since childhood has been public speaking. In seventh grade, she left the classroom during a speech given by another girl, knowing her turn was next, and she locked herself in a stall in the restroom where she stayed until the bell rang.

Thinking about this fear, Jennifer adds: "Twice – once in high school and again in college – while giving a speech, my voice shook and I sweated profusely. I saw pity in some of my classmates' eyes. Other less kind souls snickered. I had a very real and very serious phobia."

After selling her first novel, Jennifer wanted to talk to writers' groups and share her knowledge and joy. "Every cell in my body screamed at me not to do it," she says. "But I was determined, because writers are often asked to speak and give workshops. If I was going to be a writer, I needed to overcome my fear."

She practiced speaking in front of a mirror, and she learned a breathing technique that calmed her. "I decided I was going to speak to writers, fear be damned, and I did. Today, speaking before groups about writing and creativity is one of my favorite things to do."

Your Creative Frame of Mind

Once you've gotten obstacles out of the way and ended excuse making, it's time to continue creating. The right frame of mind will help you slip more easily into your creative flow. As we have discussed in previous Steps, when you're in the flow, nothing else exists but the activity in which you're engaged. Hours pass like minutes as your imagination soars and your happiness grows. But what contributes to your right frame of mind?

First, it helps if you've found the best creative outlet(s) for you – something you love that holds your interest and brings you joy. If you aren't sure what you want to do creatively, explore and play with different options. You'll know you've discovered the right activity when you find yourself completely absorbed in it. You'll love talking about it and learning from others who've been at it longer.

And this brings us to devotion, the second facet of the right frame of mind. In order to maintain your passion for the creative outlet you've chosen, you must declare you are dedicating a part of your life to it. The amount of commitment involved will be different for each individual. You might only find thirty minutes a day or an hour a week to devote to your creative pursuit, while someone else might be able to set aside six hours a day. The amount of time does not matter; it's the depth of devotion that keeps your creativity at a premium and you happy and enthusiastic.

Next, setting the mood is important. Some people create best in total silence. Others prefer background noise. Some people like to be alone, while others prefer to have the world buzzing around them. Some of us are most imaginative early in the morning. Others find their minds click into gear most smoothly after dark.

There are certain rituals that enhance atmosphere, and many individuals perform them before creative sessions.

They might light a candle, repeat an affirmation, arrange the desk, room or tools just so. Maybe they gaze out a window for a certain amount of time. The possibilities are endless and unique to the individual.

Whatever ritual you find useful, it often has profound meaning and can be a vital part of the creative process. Performing an accustomed ritual sometimes transfers you into a sort of waking-dream state that's calming, controlled, and frees your mind of self-doubts, worries, and other distractions.

The American writer John Cheever took ritual to the extreme. It's said that he dressed in a suit every morning, rode the elevator down to a basement room where he wrote, then stripped to his underwear and hung up his suit before beginning each writing session. At lunchtime, he would dress again to go upstairs, then come back to the basement after eating, undress, and get back to work. Upon finishing his writing for the day, he would dress one final time and leave.

Experiment until you find whatever helps you slip into your creative flow then return to those techniques again and again. However, keep in mind that there will be days when you just create. Jennifer sometimes writes quickly at a stop light, and Mary jots notes while exercising. The key is to find what works for you.

Step 5 Practice: Super Creative
The following Practice incorporates all we've discussed so far in this Step and will help you apply it in your creative life.

Think of a moment when you felt super creative. It may have been when you were working with one of the other Practices in this book or at another time far back in your past. Close your eyes and visualize the moment, then complete the following statements in your journal:

1. During this time that I felt super creative I was at (name the place where you were)
2. It was a.m./p.m. and I was creating a
3. I was alone/with others
4. My surroundings were noisy/quiet
5. Something else I recall about the experience is that . . .

Jennifer's Responses

1. During this time that I felt super creative I was at home in my living room.
2. It was mid-morning and I was working on my novel *The Me I Used To Be*.
3. I was alone.
4. My surroundings were quiet.
5. Something else I recall about the experience is that I was writing longhand on paper rather than typing into my computer.

Mary's Responses

1. During this time that I felt super creative I was sitting in a quiet library, using my laptop.
2. It was 10:00 a.m., and I wrote a chapter for *The Lighthouse*.

3. I was alone, except for the other library patrons.
4. It was quiet.
5. Something else I recall about the experience is that the atmosphere was solemn. I love the subject matter, and I felt self-confident because the day before I'd taken copious notes about the character.

Now read your responses again and answer these questions:
1. What component of this experience helped you be super creative?
2. At what time do you think you are the most creative? (If this is not the same time that this episode occurred, what made it different?)
3. In what sort of place do you feel the most creative? (If it is not the same type of place as this episode occurred, what made this time different?)

Mary's Responses
1. What component of your experience helped you be super creative?
The day before, I thought about the character I was going to write about and I made notes. Working in the library helped. I've always felt alive around books.
2. At what time are you the most creative? If this is not the same time that this episode occurred, what made it different?
Mornings are my high creative time because that is my high energy level time.
3. In what place do you feel the most creative? If it is not the same type of place as this episode occurred,

what made this time differ?
I do best in a quiet space where I can think.

Jennifer's Responses
1. What component of this experience helped you be super creative?
I believe that writing longhand instead of typing forced me to keep pushing forward because it's not as easy to back up and "fix" things as it is on a computer. By pushing forward, my thoughts flowed more freely without interruption.

2. At what time do you think you are the most creative? If this is not the same time that this episode occurred, what made it different?
I'm most creative late at night. There's a sort of freedom and peace of mind in knowing that that those I love most are safe in bed. However, when writing THE ME I USED TO BE I was able to be highly creative during the morning because (a) Writing longhand freed up my creative mind, and (b) I had just quit my job and I was very energized and excited about getting to stay home and spend my days as a full-time writer.

3. In what sort of place do you feel the most creative? If it is not the same type of place as this episode occurred, what made this time differ?
I feel most creative outside, however the weather doesn't often allow me to write outside. My living room has windows across one wall that look out over my front yard. I think when I sat in there while writing THE ME I USED TO BE they brought the outside inside, in a sense,

and helped me get into the flow.

Study your responses and our responses. Think about any other times when ideas flourished and you felt hyper-creative.

Do you see any repeating patterns? Was the time of day the same?

What were your surroundings? Did you perform a similar ritual? For more inspiration try new methods such as:

- Listening to music
- Taking a walk before or mid-session
- Working near water – a fountain, pond, river, lake or the ocean

All of the above have proven to help many people slip into the flow of creation. By journaling and experimenting, you will realize how to set up your ideal creative atmosphere.

Creative Happiness Journal Prompt

Write in your journal about your thoughts regarding your journey with this workshop so far. Here's a prompt if you need an idea to guide you: Write about how you might conquer the challenges you face with your creative projects.

Mary's Creative Happiness Journal

I become very creative when I go on a trip, especially if I fly. On the plane I feel like my nerves are on fire and I could create anything. I always take a notebook with me when I fly and make notes. Funny thing, when I get home and read over my notes, sometimes they don't make too much sense, yet other times I've come up with great ideas.

What I've learned from these experiences is that creativity is fun and doesn't always have to be serious and productive every single time. Just reading my writing can be joyful.

I used to think that I had to be creative-product focused all the time, and not enjoy my creative frame of mind. That is just not true. Creativity can be just for the fun of it! When I get serious, that's when I clutch and have trouble keeping my mind and thoughts lucid, and that's when my creativity suffers.

I have to have quiet when I write first drafts. When I edit I can function in noise. I need a very small space in which to create. One thing I've learned is that I don't share my creative dreams with a lot of people. I am a silent creator. Most people don't understand my creative drive and tend to dampen my spirit, so I have learned to share only with people who connect and are into creativity. And that's why I'm sharing this with you.

Jennifer's Creative Happiness Journal
In thinking about setting the mood and practicing rituals, I realize that I'm constantly altering these over time as my life circumstances change with each new project. I used to need to be completely alone in order to write. That's why I would stay up late at night after my family was in bed or I'd get up an hour early and write before they woke up.

Now my children are grown and I don't have any side jobs – I write full time. I can write any time of the day at home while my husband's at work. But after a few years of doing this, I started feeling like a hermit, getting cabin fever, and craving companionship. When you work at a job in an office, you can take a break now and then and talk to co-workers; there's a buzz of background noise – life going on around you. But when you write at home alone, you're still alone during the breaks you take and I started hating the isolation. My writing suffered because of it. So now I write at a coffee shop about three days per week.

I never thought I'd be able to slip into the flow surrounded by people and noise, but I've learned to tune everything out and on days that I need a little extra help, I slip in my ear buds and turn on my IPod. I make a music playlist for whatever book I'm writing. I choose songs that fit the mood of my story. When I listen to it, I slip more easily back into the world of my book and into the minds of the characters. However, I've found that if the music has lyrics, I'm distracted from the words in my head. So I choose instrumental music only – often from movie soundtracks. It's a lot of fun to put the soundtrack together for each book, and this has become one of my rituals.

Some other things I do from time to time that bring my ideas to the surface and help me slip into the flow – taking a walk; sitting in my backyard, weather permitting, and turning on the water in the fountain; listening to an audio soundtrack of the ocean or a trickling stream;

staring out the window.

One ritual I had to break – I used to find myself standing in my kitchen pantry eating crackers while working out a plot problem. I would be writing in my office, get stuck, and wander into the kitchen while almost in a trance. Sometimes I'd realize where I was and what I was doing and wonder how I got there. This ritual might've helped me plot but it also served to add several pounds to my backside!

Step 7

Creativity When Crisis Strikes

This Step deals with a difficult topic that may or may not apply to you at the moment, depending on current circumstances in your life. Despite the fact that the subject matter is a bit depressing, we feel it's important to discuss because, unfortunately, even if you're not currently dealing with a crisis in your life, chances are good that you have in the past or that you will at some point in the future. And when faced with a crisis, feelings of hopelessness and a sense of being overwhelmed can serve to squelch the very thing that could help you pull through the ordeal – your creativity.

If you feel this information isn't relevant to your current situation in life and are afraid it might be a downer for you to read, that's fine. Skip to Step 8 knowing that in the future, should you ever need a helping hand to assist you through a trying time when both you and your creativity are suffering, you can come back to Step 7 and find guidance.

Tough Times and Creative Perspective
Situations that result in heartache can happen slowly – a condition that builds to a crescendo – or quickly –

a disaster that jerks the floor from beneath your feet. Regardless of how the crisis occurs, it's likely that during these times of great stress and/or sadness, creating may be the last thing you feel like doing. However, as difficult as it is to believe, when you are in crisis, you may be at your highest level of creativity.

Why? Because when you face problems, you judge what is most important in your life and this forces you to tumble out of the hypnotic mode we often fall into while going through the motions of daily living. For example, the importance of facing life head-on became clear to Mary after her friend's husband died suddenly. When Mary spoke with the woman on the following day, Susan was hyper-aware of everything around her and talking about the precious nature of life. Even though she was in shock and grieving, she was in a highly creative state.

After a few weeks passed, Susan was actually able to use her grief as a creative tool and see her life with more depth and purpose. She realized she loved flowers and attended a flower arranging class. Then she went to work for a florist, and later she opened her own store.

In times of trouble, you need to believe your creativity will not desert you. This concept takes courage to accept; but if you are imagination-centered and practicing creativity, no matter what the crisis, your creativity will be pivotal and a guiding force to your happiness and healing.

However, we know that while in a crisis, the enormity of what you or a loved one are facing can make your creative interests seem frivolous and unimportant. How can you stay motivated to practice creativity when you're depressed or frightened?

Breathing Space
During a crisis, it's important to first take care of yourself. More than anything, you need rest. You need to eat healthy foods to sustain your energy. You need exercise. And you need to nurture your creativity. This is a very important step.

Creativity isn't frivolous, and it's especially important in times of trouble because it helps you thrive, and if you aren't thriving, you're of no help to anyone.

We don't mean to suggest you shouldn't take a break. It's perfectly understandable if you can't write that chapter, pick up a paint brush, go to acting class, practice playing guitar or do whatever creative things you normally do. You may need some breathing space before you dive headlong into your creative projects. If you decide to take a respite, consider using the suggested ways below to soothe your stress and stay in a creative mode.

Spend Time Outside: Even if it's only for a few minutes a day, no matter what the weather. Breathe in the fresh air. Let the sunshine warm your face and the breeze ruffle your hair. Feel the chill of the winter wind on your cheeks and the crunch of snow beneath your boots. Let your senses awaken and let yourself enjoy being alive. Nature awakens your senses and paying attention to sensory details inspires imagination. Joy may follow, even if only a little, and only for a little while.

As Mary explains, "When I'm stressed I go outside at night, stand very still and look up at the velvet sky. This easy activity helps me realize how small my problems are compared to our universe. I love being alone outside at night – there is something very mystical about it."

Listen To Soothing or Upbeat Music: Listening to music is creative because you connect musical notes and lyrics to your feelings. Plus music is inspirational, as well as a great mood-lifter. "The Effects of Musical Mood Induction on Creativity" in the *Journal of Creative Behavior*, discusses the results of a study in which seventy-one college students were exposed to different music intended to cause states of either elation, depression or neutrality. Afterward, the students who listened to music meant to inspire euphoria or depression displayed notably higher degrees of creativity than students from the neutral-music group.

Read Fiction: Reading is a great way to temporarily escape from your troubles. We've mentioned this in earlier steps – read a novel, and you become an inventor along with the author. The author's words and your own imagination work together to bring alive in your mind's eye the book's setting, the appearance of the characters, the sound of their voices, as well as a whole host of other sights, sounds, tastes, textures and scents.

Meditate: Meditation is good for your mind *and* your body. Among other health benefits, it has been shown to ease stress, lower the heart rate, increase blood flow, lower oxygen consumption and respiratory rate. Meditation, from a creative perspective, temporarily clears the mind of worries and distractions, allowing imaginative thoughts to flow more freely.

Think of other activities that soothe you and stir your imagination when your life is going well: Those same pursuits are likely to awaken and motivate your creativity during traumatic times, too.

Easing In – No Expectations

After taking a breather when you are in crisis, give yourself permission to create. If your heart and mind revolt at the thought of engaging in your creative pursuits, realize your reactions are off-center.

Tell yourself you're going to make an attempt to create because you know logically it's in your best interest – creativity brings happiness. Set aside a few minutes in the midst of the grief to pick up your pen or your paintbrush or camera, put on your apron or your tool belt.

As Mary explains, "I used to NOT create when a crisis hit my life. I moped like a tortured artist, watched mindless TV, and felt worse. Then one day I decided to 'force' myself to write after my aunt was diagnosed with a serious illness. Concentrating was difficult at first, but I made myself go through the motions of writing.

"Suddenly I was submersed in my creativity and three hours flew by. When I finished I felt relaxed, calm and ready to support my aunt. Creating helped me, and inadvertently it helped my aunt because I was calmer and happier. Now during a crisis, creativity is the first thing I turn to."

When easing back into creativity, there should be no pressure. What matters is the effort, not the outcome. Understand you may feel distracted at first, or you may not be able to maintain your concentration for long periods of time.

Accept that what you produce in these sessions might not meet your standards. All of that's okay. What's important is that you're using your imagination, and what you are looking for most is the happiness-creativity connection.

This was the case for Jennifer while seeing a loved one through a difficult challenge. She was under contract for a novel and her deadline was looming when a personal situation took place that suddenly consumed every ounce of her emotional energy and attention; she couldn't bring herself to focus on anything other than how to get through the ordeal in one piece.

For the first couple of weeks, she didn't write at all, but she started taking long walks and discovered that being outside lifted her spirits. While on these walks, sometimes she'd catch herself thinking about her novel again.

"I wasn't sure I could write, or that I even wanted to," Jennifer recalls, "but I found a little neighborhood coffee shop and decided to spend at least one hour a day there with my manuscript. It was a quiet place – most of the customers were on their laptops. It was a comforting atmosphere and felt like a safe haven. I'd been sucked dry emotionally, but as soon as I stepped through that coffee shop door, I was in my own little oasis."

At first Jennifer spent a lot of time just staring out the window, trying to think about her story, but soon she started writing again – some days only a paragraph or two, other days a complete chapter. During those brief sessions, her worries about her loved one retreated to the back of her mind and she remembered what happiness felt like.

You Are Not Alone – Transcend

Even the most highly innovative people who work in creative fields have fear and grief in their lives. They have learned to work through the difficult times and use their creativity to hold themselves up – they transcend their trying moments and problems.

Transcending the moment is a very important concept. First realize problems are going to exist whether you create or not. During times of trouble devote yourself to your creativity and become absorbed in it. Let it be the center of your truth. When hurting from a life setback or a crisis, learn to use your creativity to float above the problem.

First, embrace the fact that life problems can actually inspire you and open your mind to a new way of seeing things. If you accept this then you will have an easier time creating when times are tough.

Second, write in your Creative Happiness Journal when you are feeling down. Often, putting your problems on paper will help to clear your mind. It can also help to read the journal entries you've made in the past; these can remind you of the ways in which you've previously worked through creative issues.

The Practices and lists you've completed in this book can be of help, too. Review them when you are depressed or have a life problem, or answer all of the questions in this Step again so you might see your creative life and difficulties from a different perspective.

Third, consider having more than one creative path – a second or third creative activity that you enjoy. For instance, let's say that you make jewelry but can't seem to concentrate on designing another bracelet. If you have another creative outlet, you can turn to a different type of project. Switching gears often helps the mind relax so that even though you aren't physically designing jewelry or mentally focusing on it, your subconscious continues to work on it for you in a different way.

Step 6 Practice: Transcending Problems

Let's try a Practice to help you more fully understand the concepts we've covered in this Step. Think back to a time when you were grieving or sad, or if you're currently struggling with a difficult situation refer to it in this Practice. We realize you are probably hesitant to revisit the feelings associated with tough times, however doing so, especially if you're doing it from a safe distance, may teach you a lot about yourself – what you did or are doing right to ease your stress, and what you could/could've do(ne) better.

Close your eyes and try to feel – just for a minute – the sensations that you felt in your body. Now, in your journal, answer the following questions about that time: Did your head feel fuzzy? Did your muscles ache? Did your chest feel heavy? Did your heart hurt?

What other feelings did you experience and what did you notice about your surroundings?

Mary's Responses:
When my father was dying of prostate cancer, I noticed how beautiful the world was. His illness and the stress that went along with watching him struggle made my creative vision so sensitive I saw a bright light illuminating from his room almost every day. I was aware of rich colors and tastes and sounds. I used this situation to write one of my favorite novels, *Falling Out of Bed*.

Jennifer's Responses:
When a person I love was suffering, I suffered, too. I had a heavy feeling in my chest and a deep sadness. I felt exhausted and paralyzed. I wanted to find a way to help my loved one feel good again but didn't know how. I began to think of the situation in metaphors. My loved one's heartache became a cloud that was smothering her and squeezing out her light. I wanted to see her "shine" again. Using these metaphors, I put my feelings on paper and they became the lyrics to a song. I gave them to a musician I know, and she put them to music. Doing this gave me an outlet for my sadness.

Accepting Life Problems

Occasional problems, big or small, are a fact of life. However, if you teach yourself to create during times of crisis, you will find that creativity will bring you a smoothness of attitude, dignity and happiness. Let it work for you.

Creative Happiness Journal Prompt

Write in your journal about your thoughts regarding your journey with this workshop so far. Here's a prompt if you need an idea to guide you: Write about what you have learned about stress, sadness and creativity. Comment on times when you could not create and times you could.

Mary's Creative Happiness Journal

Long ago I was a suffering writer. If I had a problem, of course I couldn't create – I was a sensitive artist and my environment had to be at its optimum for me to produce. I learned the benefits of living creatively during a crisis, but only through trial and error.

While I was ghosting a book for a client, my best friend had a major health disaster. I greeted this problem with shock and grief. I told myself I couldn't create and be happy because it would be disrespectful to my friend because she was going through so much.

Looking back, I realize I should've admitted that my friend would not have wanted me to quit creating because she was ill. She loved that I am a writer. And me stopping creating didn't help her. I wish now that I would've embraced my friend's problem, rather than running from it. Illness touches everyone. The fact that my friend was ill had nothing to do with my creativity.

Now I know that I can create just about anywhere, any time with any problem because I've convinced myself of that fact – and my creative life is much better for it.

A few years back I learned that life isn't fair and I needed to accept that, not fight it, and create no matter what. My husband had been diagnosed with a life threatening disease. The next day I went to the college where I was teaching. I was shocked and devastated that my husband had cancer.

How could "that" happen to us? I got in the elevator to go up to the English department. I was pouty, angry and stunned. I said to one of my colleagues, "God, life isn't fair!" He looked at me and shook his head then said, "Mary, you are just now learning that fact?"

In that moment, when my creative frame of mind was at its maximum, I grabbed a hold of his statement and had an epiphany. No, life is not fair, but the way I could make it seem reasonable was to keep on with my creativity. And from that moment on, I knew I had to create during life's problems.

Jennifer's Creative Happiness Journal

Even though I know from experience that continuing to spend time pursuing my creative endeavors helps me through a crisis and brings me a measure of relief, I still struggle to do so during stressful times. I'm not sure why. Maybe because it's so hard to focus my mind on anything else but the problem. It's like that old saying, "The first step is the hardest." Sometimes that step feels more like a hurdle and it seems easier to just stay put and wallow in despair. I need to remind myself that, although the jump is painful, it's always worth it; I'll feel better for a while when I get to the other side.

Right now, I'm dealing with a lot of frustration because I'm waiting on several things to happen – things that require other people to follow through. There's very little I can do to speed them up, so I know that I should just make a better effort to concentrate on my writing for longer periods of time each day. Doing so won't make the waiting go by any faster, but it will seem like it did and I'll be happier. I know this from past experience. I'm also thinking about pursuing another creative path. That way, when my attention wanders, I can put away my writing and do something else that also requires imaginative effort.

I know my subconscious will continue to work on the book and the next time I sit down to write, the words will probably flow more smoothly. I've always wanted to learn to play an instrument again. I haven't played anything since I was a child, when I learned to play the clarinet in school band and also taught myself to play the ukulele. I would love to learn to play the violin or guitar or even the piano. The thought of trying at my age scares me a little, but it's exciting to imagine, too. Another option is taking a photography class. I am so intrigued by photographs. I even explored this interest in my novel, THROUGH HER EYES. I will give some thought to pursuing one of these things.

Step 8

Continuing Your Creative Life

Now that you have a cadre of methods to build your creativity and enhance your happiness, it's time to dig even deeper into your creative potential, find new, imaginative and joyful ways of living, and begin to flourish creatively forever.

Mind Movies – Visualization

Visualization is a method in which you imagine yourself performing a certain activity. Research supports positive visualization as an effective mental technique for producing successful results.

Many professional athletes, such as golfing sensation Tiger Woods and Olympic gold-medal swimmer Michael Phelps, reap huge benefits by incorporating the practice of visualization into their training.

In a 2008 *Golf Digest* article, Tiger's caddy at the time, Steve Williams, was quoted as saying that before shooting a 28 on the front nine holes of a Tour Championship in Florida, Tiger was "getting swing thoughts organized and the right mental picture." Williams also stated that "[…]instead of spending hours on the practice field, he [Woods] just tried to picture how he wanted to swing the club."

Similarly, Michael Phelps is said to form a mental picture of every detail of a swim, from his stroke to the sides of the pool, the night before a race.

In their book *Seeing with the Mind's Eye,* Mike and Nancy Samuels document a visualization study with basketball players practicing free throws. Three research groups were chosen at random, none of the members having any experience with visualization. Group One physically practiced free throws every day for 20 days. Group Two only practiced free throwing for two days and did NOT visualize. Group Three practiced free throwing for two days and for twenty days visualized sinking shots.

The outcome:

Group One (who practiced free throwing 20 times but did not visualize) improved 24%.

Group Three (who practiced only two times but imagined successful free throwing for 20 days) improved 23%.

Group Two (who did not visualize but practiced real free throws for two days) had 0% improvement.

The use of visualization to improve performance isn't limited to athletes. Salespeople, public speakers, actors, students and many others utilize visualization in order to reach full potential. We believe anyone can use the technique to enrich creative experiences, as well.

Actually, you probably already use this imagery method from time-to-time without even realizing it. Have you ever mentally practiced for a job interview, picturing yourself sitting across a desk from a potential employer and imagining him or her asking certain questions? Did you mentally rehearse your answers and see yourself speaking them?

Or perhaps before going on a first date, you pictured how the night would unfold and imagined yourself relaxed and having fun.

In these instances, you were mentally participating in what we call a "mind movie," and you made certain it played out in the exact way you wanted it to. As the director of and actor in this movie you felt in control, so when the actual event occurred you were prepared, relaxed and confident. This calm self-assurance helped you to perform at your best.

But how, exactly, do you go about making a mind movie? It's as simple as:

- knowing what you want to accomplish
- believing it is possible for you to accomplish it
- clearing your mind and relaxing
- picturing yourself doing the action to achieve your goal in the most optimal way.

Sensory Creative Diving (SCD)

Sensory Creative Diving is a process we use wherein Mind Movies, Sensory Details, and Creative Happiness are combined in an intensely focused way that goes beyond mere visualization.

Let's imagine you've decided to practice Sensory Creative Diving (SCD) to help you write a short story. First, you sit quietly, close your eyes, take a deep breath then picture yourself in front of your computer or at your writing table or desk.

Not only do you see yourself there, you also imagine a feeling of calm happiness coursing through your body. By setting your intention to one of joy, when you actually sit down to write, you won't consider it a chore. Plus you'll circumvent the creative anxiety that many of us often experience. In effect, you program your mind to relax and enjoy the event.

In the second step, you begin to add your five senses to the images. For touch you might conceive of pressing the computer keys and feeling the cool plastic beneath your fingertips. Or you might imagine yourself holding your pen, the weight of it in your hand and the paper against your palm.

You then conjure up the sounds of writing – the soft tap, tap, tap of the keyboard or the scratch of the pen against the white page. When you hear these familiar noises in your mind, you then go on to imagine yourself in a state of peacefulness and contentment as the words appear on either the screen or the page.

For the sense of sight, you begin to insert other visual details into the scene. These specifics will make what you're envisioning seem more real. You might imagine the clothing you're wearing while you write, the furniture in the room, what's hanging on the walls, the sight of the steam rising from the coffee cup on the table beside you.

You see and feel that you're serene as you create on the page. You even smile over something clever you've written.

In your mind's eye, you pause to lift the cup and

take a sip of the coffee. You feel the weight of the cup in your hand, the curve of the handle beneath your thumb, the slick ceramic. Taste the rich flavor of the coffee and smell the bold aroma. As you set down the mug and start writing again, you experience the zing of the caffeine when it enters your system. The words seem to flow out of you like water spilling onto the page.

As you can see, Sensory Creative Diving (SCD) helps you plunge more deeply into your sensory world and swim gently and happily through the silky waters of your imagination.

There are no limitations because SCD creates a realistic scene in your Mind Movie and you actually begin to feel as if, in that moment, you really are creating. Adding the happiness component ties that emotion to the activity, so that when you actually do create, joy is automatically triggered.

We've used the act of writing as our SCD example because that's the creative activity we know best. However, SCD can be used with any creative pursuit – cooking, sewing, fusing glass, refurbishing wood furniture – whatever it is that you do. Just remember the components: Mind Movies (visualization), utilizing all five of your senses for a deep sensory experience, and feelings of joy, peace and excitement.

Step 8 Practice: Sensory Creative Diving (SCD)
The following SCD Practice will help make this process extremely accessible to you.

Go to your journal and complete the following:

The creative activity I plan to SCD is:
For this SCD activity I will imagine myself taking the following steps and feeling happy. (List at least 3 steps, preferably more):

My Sensory Creative Diving cues will be:
1. Sight: I will see . . .
2. Sound: I will hear . . .
3. Touch: I will feel . . .
4. Smell: I will smell . . .
5. Taste: I will taste . . .

Now find a quiet place where you will NOT be interrupted, and read over your Steps and Sensory Creative Diving cues. Then take the Sensory Creative Dive. You might spend five minutes in your car doing this before you walk into your office or twenty minutes before dinner – it all depends on your schedule. The more you dive, the better you will become at it, and the more it will enhance your creative experiences later on.

Don't limit yourself to the cues and steps you wrote before attempting the exercise. If other positive sensory details find their way into your mental experience, go with them and congratulate yourself later. This means you've ventured deep into your imagination, which is the ultimate desired state of mind to be in when performing this exercise.

Jennifer's Responses
The creative activity I plan to SCD is arranging and

planting flowers in a big copper pot on my backyard patio.

For this SCD activity I will imagine myself doing these steps and feeling happy:

1. I will go to a plant nursery, find a plastic pot about the size of my copper one and put it in my basket.
2. I will wander the aisles seeking flowers and plants I like, paying attention to size and color.
3. I will experiment with placing different plants in the pot, positioning them multiple ways until I find an arrangement that pleases me.
4. At home, I will put on a hat and my gardening gloves, fill the pot with bagged soil and turn it with a trowel to break up the clumps.
5. Keeping the flowers in their containers, I will position them as I did at the store, experimenting some more until I'm pleased with the look.
6. I will remove the plants from their containers and plant them in the soil in the pot.
7. I will move the pot to the right place on the patio then sweep any spilled soil from the patio into the grass.

SCD Cues:

Jennifer's Sensory Creative Diving cues will be:

Sight: I will see all the colorful rows of flowers and plants at the nursery. I will see other people roaming the aisles and the big metal baskets they're pushing. I will see their smiles and mine. At home, I will see my patio and the pergola covering it. I will see the flowerbeds surrounding it and the big copper pot. I will see the bag of soil and the dark brown clumps spilling out of it. I will see the turquoise and copper chime hanging from the eave of the pergola. I will see my dogs, lying in the yard in the sun. I will see the yellow, pink and purple blossoms I've chosen, and the green stems and leaves beneath them.

Sound: I will hear the voices of the other customers in thenursery. I will hear the sounds of traffic on the road nearby. I will hear the soft hiss of the misting system that keeps the plants hydrated. At home, I will hear the occasional bark of one of my dogs, and the answering call of other dogs in other backyards. I will hear the melodious single note of the chime when the breeze sweeps through and brushes against it.

Touch: I will feel the moist soil between my fingers. I will feel the delicate stems of the flowers, the soft petals, the warmth of the sun on my back, the cool breeze, the happy tune running through my head.

Smell: I will smell the fragrant blossoms, spring grass.

Taste: I will taste the cinnamon gum I am chewing.

Mary's Responses

The creative activity I plan to SCD is: Styling clothing. For this activity I will imagine myself doing:

1. I will look in my closet and study my tops, skirts, pants and dresses.
2. At this point I will hum a Frank Sinatra song that matches my mood.
3. I will choose a top, pants and/or skirt, hang them together like an outfit.

4. I will add accessories: a belt, shoes, or a piece of jewelry that goes perfectly with the outfit.
5. I will put the outfit on and relish the feel of the material on my body and the way I look in it.

SCD Cues:

Mary's Sensory Creative Diving cues will be:

Sight: I will see all the rich colors and styles in my closet, my beloved hardwood floors, and my collection of belts.

Sound: I will hear the soft music I always play and experience the joyous sense of freedom it always brings me.

Touch: I will feel the soft materials against my fingertips and skin.

Scent: I will smell my mysterious Opium perfume, circling around me, making me happy.

Taste: I will taste the minty flavor of my toothpaste.

Freeing Visualization

Freeing Visualization is not as structured as Sensory Creative Diving; however, it is effective in a more subtle way and is intentional because it's planned.

For example, Tom Ford, a famous and very successful New York designer whose fashions have appeared on the red carpet at the Academy Awards many times, documents in a Vogue magazine interview (2/2012) how he takes a bath every morning and lets his mind roam.

He does this for thirty minutes every morning at approximately the same time, sipping on an iced espresso with no phone or Internet interruptions. Also, the more he does it, the better the "freeing" creativity becomes. In the interview he doesn't refer to his routine as "freeing visualization," but it clearly is, and a great example for us.

As with anything, practice usually makes us better at what we do, and Freeing Visualization is mental practice. Relaxation is a side benefit of Freeing Visualization. You simply climb into a tub of warm water, sit in your favorite chair or walk through your neighborhood and let your mind wander with the loose intention of it navigating toward your creative work.

In the next few days try Freeing Visualization and then respond to your experience in your Creative Happiness Journal. It may work for you, or you may prefer Sensory Creative Diving because it has more direction. Or come up with your own unique combination of methods. We find all of these options very effective, interchanging them on different days with different projects.

Creative Dreaming

With Creative Dreaming you set the intention of solving a problem or intensifying your creativity before you fall asleep, believing you will be more creative or have an answer when you wake.

Creative Dreaming isn't about *actually dreaming* the answer to a problem, although this does occasionally happen. In this complex phenomenon, the power of suggestion works on your mind at a subconscious level while you are sleeping.

When you make a suggestion to yourself before

you fall asleep or suggest solving a problem, your mind goes to work while you rest, searching for answers and possibilities in the maze of your subconscious. Often, the answer springs forth as soon as you wake because dreaming, whether you remember your dreams or not, is a form of imagination.

When you allow yourself to create at this subconscious level, you intentionally dedicate and consign yourself to your creativity with a deeper commitment, and your awareness in the morning might surprise you.

Another form of Creative Dreaming is simply becoming more aware of what you are thinking in the moments just after you wake. First thoughts have a tendency to disappear as the day falls into your life, so many people place a pad of paper and a pen on their nightstand and jot down their thoughts before they get out of bed.

For many years, Mary has practiced noting her first thoughts of the morning. Sporadically, she has insight into a life challenge or creative problem when she wakes, and she makes a note of it.

In Mary's own words, it happens this way: "I wake and it's as if my inner voice speaks to me. Weird, I know, but many times I've come up with a solution to a challenge – and all solutions are creative. Ideas for solving my friends' dilemmas even come to me during that first waking time.

I don't have to jot down these thoughts because I've trained myself to be aware of them and I remember. It's as if my subconscious voice wakes me up with one sentence that is very poignant. For example, the other day, a writer friend asked me about a plot point she was working on. That afternoon I couldn't come up with an idea for her, yet the next morning, the moment I woke, an idea popped into my mind, 'She should make the character not want to move,' and this suggestion worked for her."

The more you "listen" and expect these first waking epiphanies, the more often you will experience them. However, you can't force or will them to happen. Just relax and be aware.

Encouraging Serendipity, Luck and Creative Irony. . . Oh, My!

The standard definition for serendipity is "luck, chance or good fortune." But the definition in relation to creativity is more complex. Creativity involves irony – you, the creator, look at something everyone sees, but you envision it differently, with fresh surprise. That's creative irony, which many interpret as luck or serendipity.

Many people wonder if divine participation is at work when someone has a creative epiphany that seems miraculous. We tend to believe that these occurrences come about only through the hard work of the receiver, either consciously or unconsciously. This person has been practicing her creative art, paying attention to the world around her with her five senses, and is open to irony.

So how has luck gotten such good press concerning creativity? Luck, to the non-creator, seems like the best answer because it requires no recognition of hard work and talent. For some people – usually those who aren't practicing their creativity – it's difficult to understand that practicing creativity brings results. And if you can credit luck, then a creative person doesn't deserve any praise for her accomplishments.

We couldn't disagree more with that mindset. As Louis Pasteur stated, "Chance favors the prepared mind."

So what is the prepared mind? Practice and a life structured with enough space so that when opportunities arise or "accidents" happen, they're recognized. Put another way, you have to have a fluid life so that when ironic incidents flow in, you notice them. In a rigidly structured life, it's difficult for those accidents to march in because there's no room for them.

To encourage an abundance of creative irony in your life, do these three things:

1. Notice every day how things are connected. For example, you see a photo of a skyscraper and you are aware enough to notice its design could be replicated in a piece of jewelry.

2. Be curious, inquisitive and brave enough to follow your curiosity around a corner. For example, you read how designer Tom Ford freely visualizes every morning, and you try doing the same, even though you are a little skeptical it will work.

3. Relax and have a good time. This is self-explanatory.

With all of the above, you train your eyes and ears to notice serendipity or creative irony. Because when serendipity happens – a so-called accident takes place – we need to pay attention and notice if we're to reap the benefits. How lucky is that?

Burnt-out Creatives

Anyone who is perpetually creative, either through their work or hobbies, may find themselves in an imaginative recession or feel as if their creativity is slipping away. We call these people burnt-out creatives, and you may be one of them.

As we touched on in Steps 6 and 7, stress, responsibility, tragedy, sadness, disappointment, or working too hard toward your creative goals can serve to snuff out a creative person's drive and leave her feeling as imaginative as a cold puddle of wax.

We have both experienced being burnt-out creatives. Jennifer experienced burn out and went into a writing slump when family stresses and too much work impinged on her life.

Mary experienced burn out while teaching four college courses, working on her Ph.D. and writing a novel on deadline for her publisher.

If you are a creative person who knows she is creative yet is now experiencing burn out, the exercises in this book will help you to find your creative spirit again. You need to look at your creativity as play instead of work. Yes, sometimes when you create for a living it feels like drudgery, the hardest work ever, and if you constantly think of it as that, then you probably will burn out and will not experience creative joy.

The key to not burning out is to pace yourself and realize you are not superhuman. Creativity needs room to breathe and grow or it will fade like sunlight at dusk from too much work and stress. Additionally, creativity needs a fun component.

When Jennifer feels burned out and in a funk she engages in a creative activity different from writing fiction. She'll also switch up her routine to re-engage her right brain, schedule a creative play date with herself, or try one or more of the Practices in this book.

When Mary is burned out, she makes herself take a much needed break and then she will refocus on how she can look at her work as fun. For example, when she was working toward her doctorate, she continually told herself that research was her passion and that she was enjoying the reading and writing. And soon it did become a joy.

Are you a burnt-out creative?

If your answer is "Yes" then write in your journal about why you burned out. Then jot down some ideas of how you can manage the stress of creating too much.

If you are a burnt out creative, the Practices in this book will make you realize that creativity should not be continually serious. You need to take a break (if you possibly can) and find the joy in your creativity again. All of our Practices will help you, and refocusing will ignite the creative flame once again.

Creative Anxiety

When we are in a highly creative mode, whether it's taking photographs, scrapbooking, making up metaphors or painting, our awareness spikes. Physically our pupils narrow, our hearts beat a little faster, our breath becomes shallow, and we experience a heightened consciousness.

Rollo May, humanistic psychologist, postulates that

this keen consciousness is the same response as the flight or fight response humans have when they are in threatening situations. With these intense feelings, new creatives read their physical responses as anxiety and/or fear.

When children create they have no fear because the fear reaction to physical changes has not been learned. A child's response to creativity is one of joy – giggling and dancing, energy coursing through their bodies. However, when adults create they sometimes experience an odd reaction, becoming overwhelmed with what they think are anxious feelings.

As a creative person, you need to teach yourself these reactions are not anxiety but the joy of self actualizing your potentialities. And you can do this in other areas of your life beyond the creative, as well.

For example, a few months ago Mary decided she wanted to ride a roller coaster just for the experience. As the time to ride drew nearer, she began having physical reactions to the idea of riding a roller coaster, something new to her, and told her husband she wasn't going because she was afraid.

Her husband, a retired fighter pilot, studied her for a moment and said, "That's not fear you're feeling; it's excitement."

Mary thought about his statement for a few days then decided he was right. Her fearful physical response to riding a roller coaster was the same as when she experiences excitement – her heart beating faster, butterflies in her stomach, and a jumpy feeling gliding over her body. So instead of being fearful of riding a roller coaster, she decided she was lucky to ride one and should feel excited about it and then, suddenly, she was.

"Funny, I had used this same method to get over fear of public speaking," Mary recalls. "When I first began giving presentations about creative writing and creativity, I was apprehensive. After thinking about my reactions, I flipped my interpretation of my physical responses, telling myself I wasn't afraid but excited about speaking to a group of people who wanted to hear what I had to say about creativity and writing. When I did this, I sparkled on stage and really enjoyed myself."

Did Mary ride the roller coaster? Yes. Every time she felt that zing of what she thought was fear, she told herself it was excitement and smiled. She attached her physical reactions to joy instead of fear, and her anxiety disappeared. Did she enjoy the ride? "Of course," says Mary. "And I'll do it again."

As Rollo May states, "Anxiety comes from not being able to know the world you're in, not being able to orient yourself in your own existence," or simply put, understanding your physical reactions and attaching them to a different mental reaction.

This brings us to the reason why the creative act is confusing and sometimes feels anxiety-ridden. When we create, we are making order out of chaos and our sense of identity seems threatened. The world is not as we experienced it before we began to create. To most humans this is confusing, and that makes it seem scary. We are no longer who we were.

Step 8 Practice: Creative Anxiety Be Gone

Let's do a Practice that will help you understand your "anxiety" about trying new activities, creative or otherwise.

Think about a time when you were nervous about doing something new. Close your eyes and feel the same feelings you felt. Then complete these statements in your journal:

1. I felt anxious when I was . . .
2. Emotionally I felt . . .
3. My physical reactions were . . .

Read your responses, then close your eyes and make yourself feel the physical reactions that you felt when you were anxious. Then create a Mind Movie where you are smiling at your reactions and shaking your head over them because you know they are a part of being excited about your creativity.

Next, write in your Creative Happiness Journal about your creative excitement.

Jennifer's Responses

I felt anxious when I was asked to give a workshop to a group of 8th graders and it was the first time I'd spoken to that age group.

Emotionally I felt lacking in the skills I thought I needed to engage with this age group. I was nervous, self-conscious, and fearful that I wouldn't be able to hold their attention.

My physical reactions were a rapidly beating heart, difficulty catching my breath, lightheadedness, and a flushed face until I became more comfortable.

Mary's Responses
I felt anxious when I started writing my new novel. I wondered if I could complete the task.

Emotionally I felt as if I were about to cry. I want to be creative, yet at times, it's like facing a block wall that I just want to smash with words.

My physical reactions were stereotypical. My stomach had butterflies, my skin felt extra sensitive and my head pounded.

Every person who attempts to create will experience creative disruption. The best thing to do is acknowledge you feel this way, and use the methods we've discussed to overcome or circumvent it.

Another good thing to do: Think of all the creative people in this world and how we keep creating every day, despite ourselves.

Creative Happiness Journal Prompt
Write in your journal about your thoughts regarding your journey with this workshop so far. Here's a prompt if you need an idea to guide you: Respond to your feelings about creative excitement. Also document your experience with Sensory Creative Diving (SCD) and other methods that you are using or planning to use.

Mary's Creative Happiness Journal
I have practiced Mind Movies or visualization almost all

my life. I'm a big daydreamer and I love to sit and look out a window and just imagine things. When Jennifer and I created Sensory Creative Diving (SCD) I could see the pieces of mind movies, sensory details and creative happiness coming together as if it were a beautiful puzzle, and all the pieces fit together perfectly to form this wonderful tool to enhance creativity and happiness.

When I do Sensory Creative Diving it's like taking a vacation. Even if I'm upset, depressed or just in a funk, I can move myself out of those moods by imagining positive, creative events. It's like a wonderful vacation that doesn't cost anything except a little bit of time.

I'm a great fan of Tom Ford the designer, and when I read his interview about visualizing in the bathtub every morning I felt like I'd met a friend. No wonder he's so creative and happy. Freeing Visualization is like an isometric exercise for the mind.

Creative Anxiety is so interesting, and I've overcome a lot of mine by working in a creative field. When I get anxious I tell myself it's only feelings and my feelings can be changed. Now I enjoy that hyped-up feeling I get when I begin to create – how exciting it is to invent something.

Jennifer's Creative Happiness Journal

I experience creative anxiety every time I start a new book. It feels like a mix of excitement and fear. I love my new story idea and can't wait to watch it come alive on the page, but I'm also afraid that I won't be able to make what I'm imagining as vivid in words as it is in my mind. No matter how many books I write and publish, no matter how many compliments on them I receive by word of mouth or in reviews, I still go through this with every new book. The trick is to just get started putting words down. To do this, I've learned to visualize the words as the ingredients for clay. Once I have them all assembled and mixed, I can then begin to shape and carve them into that beautiful thing I'm imagining. In other words, the finished book is the finished sculpture. This works to trick me into starting because clay doesn't have to be perfect – it's just a blob – so the words I write initially don't have to be perfect, either. I'm able to get started and my fear gradually fades and the excitement takes over as I become caught up in the flow of my work and forget about everything else.

It also helps to visualize myself carrying out my writing session for the day. Sometimes I do this through journaling early in the morning and stating how the session is going to play out. I write things such as: *Today I will get into the flow of my story quickly. The real world will fall away from me and I will be in Lily's world, seeing what she sees and experiencing all of her other senses. I will feel her emotions, hear her thoughts and I will transfer it vividly to the page. The writing will spill from my fingers onto the page and I will move the story forward quickly and smoothly.*

As I'm writing these words in my journal, I visualize myself in front of my computer during my session for the day. I am always amazed by how much this process helps my creativity whenever I practice it.

Celebrate!

Congratulations! By completing this workshop, you have taken enormous steps toward becoming the balanced, happy, creative being you are meant to be. It's our sincere hope that you take what you've learned, put it to work for you in your daily life, and grasp all the bliss that is yours for the taking.

Let your creativity give you wings and take flight!